"With the precision of a learned theologian and the heart of a wise, guiding pastor, Gene Tempelmeyer's *The Passover Mystery* helps us recover a sense of awe, reverence, understanding, and application of this mystery to our journey as followers of Christ. As I slowly and carefully read his sage words, I came away with a deep sense of all four of those dimensions, and I am grateful for having done so."

—JEFF CROSBY,
author of *The Language of the Soul*

"Pithy and insightful—'The cross is good news even before the resurrection'—don't even consider starting it without a highlighter."

—MARLENE LEFEVER,
Christian educator

"The Passover mystery reads as part memoir, part theological treatise, drawing on Tempelmeyer's personal and decades-long pastoral experience to reframe the meaning and impact of the cross of Jesus in profoundly hopeful and helpful ways for our lives and society today."

—SCOTT MOORE,
executive director, Youth Unlimited (YFC Toronto)

"For many Christians, the cross has been reduced to being a 'fix' for sin, resulting in a faith that wearily strives for perfection, while internally, their experience is heavy, shame filled, and dry. Tempelmeyer's recovery of the ancient Christian understanding of Jesus as the Passover Lamb is full of hope, transforming our faith from drudgery to adventure. Rather than an exit strategy from a failing earth, God invites us into his work of making a whole new world."

—SAM CHAISE,
executive director, Christie Refugee Welcome Centre

"Weaving together a rich discussion of historical context and biblical exegesis, Tempelmeyer reconnects the Passover and the cross, God's promise to Abraham and Pentecost. The result is an explosive mix which challenges us to rethink our understanding of God's work on the cross. Delivered with a vulnerable and gentle pastoral heart, Tempelmeyer opens up the possibility of a fresh new engagement of the gospel with a disillusioned culture."

—DONALD GOERTZ,
Tyndale University, retired

The Passover Mystery

The Passover Mystery

How the Cross Creates a New Human

Gene Tempelmeyer

RESOURCE *Publications* • Eugene, Oregon

THE PASSOVER MYSTERY
How the Cross Creates a New Human

Copyright © 2022 Gene Tempelmeyer. All rights reserved. Except for brief quotations in critical publications or reviews, no part of this book may be reproduced in any manner without prior written permission from the publisher. Write: Permissions, Wipf and Stock Publishers, 199 W. 8th Ave., Suite 3, Eugene, OR 97401.

Resource Publications
An Imprint of Wipf and Stock Publishers
199 W. 8th Ave., Suite 3
Eugene, OR 97401

www.wipfandstock.com

PAPERBACK ISBN: 978-1-6667-3759-2
HARDCOVER ISBN: 978-1-6667-9719-0
EBOOK ISBN: 978-1-6667-9720-6

APRIL 15, 2022 8:34 AM

Scripture quotations are from the New Revised Standard Version Bible, copyright © 1989 National Council of the Churches of Christ in the United States of America. Used by permission. All rights reserved worldwide. NSRVBibles.org.

Scripture quotations marked (NIV) are taken from the Holy Bible, New International Version®, NIV®. Copyright © 1973, 1978, 1984, 2011 by Biblica, Inc.™ Used by permission of Zondervan. All rights reserved worldwide. www.zondervan.comThe "NIV" and "New International Version" are trademarks registered in the United States Patent and Trademark Office by Biblica, Inc.™

Scripture taken from The Voice™. Copyright © 2012 by Ecclesia Bible Society. Used by permission. All rights reserved.

Contents

The Mystery of the Cross | vii

1. WHERE IS THE LAMB? | 1
2. PASSOVER | 10
3. ONE NEW HUMANITY | 22
4. FORGIVENESS | 34
5. GETTING BACK ON TRACK | 47
6. AGONY | 61
7. A NEW WORLD BEGINS | 68
8. THE GOSPEL | 78

Bibliography | 95

The Mystery of the Cross

> For people who are stumbling toward ruin, the message of the cross is nothing but a tale of fools by a fool. But for those of us who are already experiencing the reality of being rescued [and made right], it is nothing short of God's power.
>
> —1 Corinthians 1:18, The Voice New Testament

We drive through the city. Suddenly, between high-rise apartment buildings, we catch a glimpse of a steeply pitched roof. Perched on its tallest peak is a cross. Immediately we know this is a Christian church, meaning there are followers of Jesus in this community. Nothing so readily declares the presence of Christians as a cross.

If the apostle Paul is correct that the message of the cross is "nothing short of God's power," we had better understand its meaning and significance. But having a doctrine of the cross and possessing its power in our own experience may be two quite different things. If we are not, in fact, "already experiencing the reality of being rescued," it may well be because we have too limited an understanding of what the cross of Jesus means and did.

Understanding the cross is like peeling an onion. There are many layers of meaning in the curious death of Jesus.

We may, for example, want to ask about the historical significance of the cross. We have sanitized the cross on top of our buildings to such an extent that seldom would a person pause on the sidewalk and ponder why that building is emblazoned with an image of torture and execution. Imagine the questions that might be asked if, for example, a building were constructed in your neighborhood featuring a large, stylized gallows and noose. Or an electric chair. Or a guillotine.

This is, in part, why I describe the death of Jesus on a cross as curious.

What do you think of Nelson Mandela? I have noticed how the answer to that question shifts when the person asked happens to be white, from South Africa, and to have lived through the breakdown of apartheid. One person's hero is another person's terrorist. And, perhaps more commonly, yesterday's terrorist becomes today's hero.

It was not only the Pharisees who built tombs and decorated the monuments of righteous prophets killed by their fathers. As Jesus suggested of Pharisees in his time, I suspect most of us are convinced we would not have joined our fathers in killing those who confronted our collective sin with great force.

The cross was developed by Romans as punishment for only two classes of criminal: slaves who had run away or otherwise seriously offended their master, and political insurgents. The brutality of crucifixion insured that the most marginalized would rather accept their lot in life than risk the consequences of seeking justice and freedom. For those familiar with the Hunger Games trilogy, the cross served exactly the same purpose as those cruel games: to remind the powerless how truly powerless they actually were.

What does it say about Jesus of Nazareth that this was the way he died? We know he wasn't a slave. What did the Roman government of Judea think he was? What does it say about his first followers that the literal scandal of his death became essential to their central message of hope? What does it say about us that we have made our symbolic crosses so clean that it is difficult to be reminded by their presence that Jesus was executed as a criminal by a religious elite and an occupying empire?

The Mystery of the Cross

Why that particular death? Why a cross? What is the historical significance of the cross to our belief and way of living?

Moving beyond the purely historical meaning of the cross, what is the spiritual and theological significance of the cross? How does a cruel Roman execution continue to have an impact on our own spiritual reality?

The theological word for the answer to this question is "atonement." Understanding a concept often best begins by exploring the words used to describe it. In their letters, both Paul and John use Greek words that share a common root to get at the idea of atonement. These words might be translated "expiation" or "propitiation" and quite likely need definition from the English as much as from the Greek.

As Paul uses this Greek word, it refers to the place and means of forgiveness. It may refer specifically to the "mercy seat" in the Old Testament tabernacle and temple, where sacrifices were offered. The cross of Jesus now becomes the mercy seat: the place we can go knowing we can certainly find God's compassion and forgiveness there.

John uses the word in a slightly different form. In John's writing the focus is on the act of God giving his mercy: God finding a way to initiate and offer compassionate forgiveness. It may be important to note that John does not identify the cross specifically as the act generating atonement. Rather, John sees Jesus in his totality as the means of atonement (1 John 2:2, NRSV).

The Greek root word shared by John and Paul, *hileos*, ironically, refers to being cheerful. The words used by John and Paul imply that the mercy of God is what reconciles us to God. The grief of separation and isolation are over, and both we and God can be cheerful now because a mutually loving relationship has been restored. All this New Testament thought points back to Old Testament experiences, rituals, and ideas.

For John, atonement is not so much a doctrine as it is a way of life. Renewed relationship with God gives us a new cheerfulness in the face of our difficulties and even our sins. Freed from our sins and the principle of sin itself, we are, in the words of Paul, now able to "walk in newness of life" (Romans 6:4, NRSV).

What did the death of Jesus on a cross do to make this happen? How does the historical event of Jesus of Nazareth dying via public execution at the hands of Roman occupiers and his own religious leaders free us from the oppression of sin? How did the cross reach back in history to connect with and continue God's work and covenant with the Jewish people? And how does the cross reach forward in history to connect us to that freedom and relationship with God? All of this raises the question: What is the problem that requires us to be reconciled to God in the first place?

For roughly a millennium, the church has espoused a view of the cross that is almost exclusively limited to saving Christian believers from the possibility of hell and getting them into heaven when they die. In this framework, such salvation is achieved by Jesus standing in the place of sinful humanity, voluntarily enduring all the violent rage God would heap on us for our sinfulness.

The New Testament seems to carry a much broader view of the cross. In the New Testament, followers of Jesus join our Lord at Golgotha as we carry our own crosses in obedience to him. Among New Testament believers, our continuing service to God completes what remains to be completed by the cross. The cross is offered as an example to us by which we may participate in the renewal of the universe.

I believe three things about the cross: (1) the cross works as one part of a larger sequence of events that includes the birth, life, teaching, burial, resurrection, and ascension of Jesus; (2) Jesus's death by Roman execution at the hands of his own leaders and his resurrection from the tomb three days later is *the* pivot point of history; and (3) unless such beliefs move from our heads into our hearts, spirits, and way of life, we will not be able to say with Paul, "We are already experiencing the reality of being rescued." Atonement must be more than a belief. It must become an essential part of our identity, self-understanding, and response to others.

Very early in Christian history the idea of "The Pascal Mystery" entered the liturgy and thought of the church. Incorporating the life, death, resurrection, and ascension of Christ into one broad act by which we are reconciled with God, the Passover (Pascha) Mystery identifies the execution of Jesus with the Passover Lamb rather than the lamb sacrificed as a sin offering on the Day of Atonement.

This book suggests that returning to that early doctrine would change our understanding of the cross, God, and our own humanity. The Paschal mystery reconciles us to a God who has always loved us. Further, being a product of human anger rather than divine anger, the cross reconciles us to one another and to ourselves, freeing us from the pain and guilt of our own histories. The Passover Mystery nourishes and sustains God's people on their journey to freedom and wholeness.

1

Where Is the Lamb?

A father and son were hiking up a mountain together. Their intention, upon reaching the peak, was to complete a religious ceremony such as the father had experienced in his homeland many years before and many miles away. The son knew this ceremony would end with a sacrifice from his father's large flocks of livestock. As they climbed, however, he became increasingly puzzled and concerned.

Finally, he asked, "Dad, where is the lamb?"

"God will provide what we need," his father answered.

We can only guess what the son thought of this answer. It was the kind of thing his father was always saying. In fact, the son knew that his mom and dad had tried to have a baby for a long time without success, and that, despite their very advanced age, his mom had finally become pregnant with him. He knew how much he meant to his parents and how they considered his very existence a miraculous gift to them.

But he must have wondered what would happen on the mountain peak. Would they actually find a lamb there? Would his dad be disappointed by unrealistic religious expectations?

The answer turned out to be far more frightening that his father's potential disappointment. His father had meant to sacrifice him, Isaac, all along.

The Passover Mystery

I have worked as a pastor all my adult life. This means my kids grew up listening to me preach every Sunday. My daughter has always said that she would prefer to hear me speak than any of the other preachers she has heard. I receive this compliment understanding that it mostly has to do with familiarity and affection. But about the time she was finishing high school, I gave a sermon about Abraham offering his son Isaac as a sacrifice to God.

On the ride home she blurted, "Dad, I hate it when you talk about that story!"

"What? Why?"

"Do you know how disconcerting it is to hear your father describe someone willing to kill their kid for God? When I know you love God and think you should try to do what he says!?"

Point taken. This is truly an awful story. For a very long time I missed the point.

Abraham had grown up in the plain between the Tigris and Euphrates Rivers in the ancient empire of Mesopotamia. He had grown up among people who came to believe in an angry and cruel god named Molech. To appease this Molech's anger and earn his favor, Molech's followers offered sacrifices. If a worshiper really wanted to impress Molech, they would offer a human sacrifice. The highest, most significant sacrifice one could offer was one's own child.

On top of that mountain Abraham was only doing what he had seen performed by deeply religious people when he was younger. He was following sacred tradition.

This is precisely why God had called Abram to leave his nation, his home, and his family. God meant to launch an entire movement of human redemption through Abram. All the violence and anger of the world was to be replaced by blessing and love. To do this, God would have to wean Abram from the beliefs and religious practice of his youth. The point of this old story is not that a father should be willing to kill his child for God, but that God would never want or accept such a sacrifice.

The Bible is an honest record of a community of people who tried to understand, love, and obey God. They didn't always get it right. But through their efforts, even mistaken efforts at times, God was showing them who God really is and what God really wants. Abraham's aborted attempt to sacrifice Isaac is one of these learning and reframing experiences God designed to clarify what it means to believe in and serve God.

The Old Testament is full of prohibitions against human sacrifice, particularly the sacrifice of children. Psalm 106 goes so far as to suggest that such sacrifices are not inspired by God but by demons, and that to offer such a sacrifice is to make demons into gods. Only a demon would have such a wickedly destructive agenda as to require so unloving an act.

That God prevented Abraham from killing Isaac did not entirely mitigate the destructiveness of Abraham's willingness to do so. After this incident Abraham and Sarah, his wife, never appear together again. Sarah moves elsewhere, and when she dies Abraham has to travel to Kiriath-Arba to bury her there.

The Midrash is a collection of writings that fill in gaps or provide explanations that careful reading of the Torah, the Old Testament, requires. Jewish scholars regard these ancient commentaries as sacred text. The Midrash relates how Sarah moved to Kiriath-Arba, where she died of a broken heart because, in a sense, she stood to lose both her husband and her son on the same day. The mournful sound of the *shofar*, the Jewish horn, is said to contain the tears of Sarah.

Upon hearing of her husband's intent to sacrifice their beloved son, Sarah could no longer bring herself to live with him. Sarah saw eye to eye with my daughter on this matter.

How would you judge the morality of sacrificing a child?

I once had a congregant whose son was drafted into the US Army during the Vietnam War. She begged him to flee to Canada, where she held citizenship. His name is now engraved in the Vietnam Memorial in Washington, DC. It is difficult to imagine sending a child to war. But I can understand a parent being willing to do so out of loyalty to a worthy cause. Nevertheless, even though I recognize his religious history and culture, I truly cannot

3

understand on any kind of personal level Abraham's willingness to offer his son as a sacrifice to God.

It might be argued that God is not bound by the moral values we have developed. While this is true, it is also true that the moral values that should guide people of faith are based on God's own character and behavior. The consistent principle of holiness is summarized in the law of Moses, "Be holy, for I am holy" (Leviticus 11:44 NRSV). Jesus reiterates this principle when he rejects the wisdom of his spiritual ancestors:

> You have heard that it was said, "You shall love your neighbor and hate your enemy." But I say to you: "Love your enemies and pray for those who persecute you, that you may be children of your Father in heaven; for he makes the sun rise on the evil and on the good, and sends rain on the righteous and on the unrighteous." (Matthew 5:43-45 NRSV)

Many families develop their own games to play on long road trips. One of the games my family enjoyed was writing new verses to a song my dad used to sing us at bedtime. I have no idea where he learned it. The chorus went:

> *Young folks, old folks, everybody come,*
> *Come to the Sunday School and make yourselves at home.*
> *Please leave your razor blades and chewing gum at the door,*
> *And I'll tell you Bible stories like you've never heard before.*[1]

This was followed by a humorous or satiric retelling of a Bible story. One of our favorites was Moses thinking he was going to drown all the while he was floating in a basket down the Nile. Another was about Daniel surviving the lions' den because he was a dentist and he pulled the lions' teeth. Of all those my father had learned, our favorite of all was one we composed for ourselves on a road trip to see our grandparents.

> *God said to Abraham, "You'd better kill your son."*
> *Abraham thought that might be a lot of fun.*

---

[1]. Author unknown (public domain). This ditty is known by a number of titles with an even greater number of wordings.

WHERE IS THE LAMB?

But it gave the people in the town below quite a jolt,
So they put him in a chair with fifty thousand volts.

My point in reciting this—possibly irreverent—ditty is that I am always astounded how we drop our moral filters when we read Bible stories. If someone in your church came to believe God was telling them to kill one of their children as a sacrifice to God, how would you respond? If you heard on a news broadcast that someone had killed their child in a religious ceremony, what would you think should happen to that parent?

Does the fact that an incident took place many years ago or that it was recorded in the Bible make any difference to its morality? It further astounds me that it is often those people who protest most loudly against moral relativity who most readily assert the moral validity of things that happen in the Bible and defend biblical characters for doing things we would jail them for today.

When reading a passage about an act or event that we would condemn today on the basis of Christian morality, we need to recognize that the story is honestly given as a cautionary tale to carry our collective morality further. The story of tensions in the family of Jacob, a family that included two wives who happened to be sisters, serves as an example of why polygamy should be rejected. Just so the story of Abraham offering Isaac serves as a warning against the utter immorality of offering human and child sacrifices. To the careful reader, the consequent separation of Abraham and Sarah seals this message.

As I processed my daughter's discomfort with my retelling of the story of Isaac, I had to recognize a growing discomfort within myself. My discomfort was not only with Abraham's willingness to sacrifice Isaac. I became equally uncomfortable with what I believed about another father sacrificing a beloved son.

"Where is the lamb?" Many years and generations later John the Baptist pointed his followers to Jesus of Nazareth with an answer to Isaac's pressing question: "Here is the Lamb of God who takes away the sin of the world!" (John 1:29 NRSV).

What does this mean? How does this work? What kind of sacrifice was Jesus? In the final analysis, was he killed by his own

Father? It is interesting to observe that John did not predict that Jesus would become God's lamb upon his death. Rather, walking around the area of the wilderness where John was meeting with crowds who had come to see him, Jesus was already the Lamb of God and already taking away the sins of the world.

Between Abraham and John the Baptist, Jewish ritual solved Isaac's riddle about the lamb in a number of ways. There were many lambs sacrificed by people of the Old Testament, often meaning different things and working in different ways.

What would we find if we looked at Jewish patterns and understanding of animal sacrifice without layers of Christian thought and assumption guiding us? If we dealt only with the Scripture verses describing Levitical sacrifices, we would come up with a very different notion of what such sacrifice means and, consequently, what the cross of Jesus would have meant to a Jewish person before the destruction of the temple in AD 70.

The Talmuds are ancient Jewish collections of Scripture, midrashim (the plural of "midrash"), rabbinic ideas, and interpretations of the Old Testament, carrying considerable authority in Jewish thought. Reading the Old Testament and the Talmud offers us a pretty good idea of how the sacrificial system actually worked.

Qorbanot is Hebrew for "sacrifices." The root of this word means "to draw near." Forgiveness of sin was not the main point of Jewish sacrifice. Sacrifices were offered as a way of drawing near to God. Some sacrifices dealt with sin, and all sacrifices were in some way a resolution of sin in that forgiveness removes hesitation and doubt that would otherwise prevent the offerer from drawing near to God. But many sacrifices had nothing to do with sin in a direct way.

There were five categories of sacrifice:

1. *Olah*, the "burnt offering," was a sacrifice symbolizing one's total and complete willingness to submit to and obey God. Unlike most sacrifices, no part of the animal offered was to be eaten. This sacrifice of a complete animal represented the willingness of the one offering such a sacrifice to give everything one had and everything one was to God. It was

a sacrifice about intention for the future rather than guilt or shame from the past.

2. *Zebakh shelamim*, the "peace offering," sounds like the most fun of the sacrifices. We might consider it the tailgate party of the Old Testament. A bit of the animal was offered to God by burning it on the altar. But most of the meat was eaten. A portion was reserved for the priest, while the rest became a barbecue for the person offering the sacrifice along with their friends and family. This offering was a celebration of community and family and was an offering of gratitude for both. By burning some of the meat on the altar, God actively and materially was participating in the community barbecue.

3. *Asham*, the "guilt offering," was a "just in case" provision. Generally, one would make a guilt offering if one was not certain whether a sin had been committed. This was particularly applied to a possible breach of trust. If one made a guilt offering and later discovered somehow that one's suspected sin was indeed a real sin, one would then be required to also offer a "sin offering" (as described below.) The cooked meat from a guilt offering went entirely to the priest(s).

4. *Minkhah*, a "food and drink" offering, was given much the same way we celebrate Thanksgiving or Harvest Sunday in North America. This might be an offering of grain, wine, or livestock that was the product of a farmer's labor. The offering was an expression of gratitude for God's provision even in the things one provided for oneself. Some of the offering would be fully burned on the altar as a gift to God, while other parts of the offering were given for the priest's use.

5. Finally, *khatat*, the "sin offering," is the sacrifice most frequently identified with the cross in the last millennium of Western Christianity. The name of this offering comes from the Hebrew word *khatat*, meaning "to miss the mark." The sin offering represented confession of sin, remorse, and a desire to reestablish a relationship with God. Some forms of sin offering were personal, but there were many communal sin

offerings that took into account the reality that, more often than not, there has been a community influence in an individual's sin. Indeed, there were times when the whole community sinned together and individual guilt resulted simply from being part of a sinful system. As with the guilt offering, the meat from the sin offering was given to the priest(s).

The sin offering was made only in a handful of special circumstances:

- On the Day of Atonement, when the high priest entered the holiest place, to protect the high priest's life
- Upon the appointment of a new priest
- Upon the termination of a Nazirite vow (a vow to live under a variety of ascetic rules to maintain a special closeness to God)
- After recovery from a skin disease, which was generally seen as a punishment for sin, particularly for the sin of slander
- After childbirth, menstruation, or abnormal bodily discharge, all of which were seen to imply a temporary, unintentional marital separation. Such a sacrifice would be offered by both husband and wife.

The rabbis were clear that a sin offering would only be valid for unintentional sin. Intentional and malicious sins could not be atoned for by sacrifice. Such sin required a combination of prayer and *tzedakah* (acts of charity and good deeds). Intentional sins could only be offset by repentance—that is, changed behavior—and reaching out to God to restore relationship with him.

The offering of these sacrifices was a way for ancient Hebrews to invite and experience God in the totality of their lives. It was about work, gratitude, commitment, marriage, food, family, friendship, and failure. The sacrifice invited God's active participation into every corner of life, making every aspect of life sacred.

The apostle Paul alludes to this when he urges Roman believers: "Present your bodies as a living sacrifice, holy and acceptable to God, which is your spiritual worship" (Romans 12:1).

Where Is the Lamb?

From the very start of Jewish history, God revealed himself to our father Abraham as wholly different from the gods worshiped in Abram's Chaldean world. Those gods were demanding and angry. They required human sacrifice: sometimes to the extent of one's own child.

God wanted to teach Abraham what kind of God he actually is. So he tested Abraham by asking him to take his son and offer him as Abraham had seen done at home in Chaldea. Or, perhaps, God merely did not intervene when Abraham felt compelled to make an offering such as he had seen in his homeland. In either case, when they came to the top of the mountain God had already provided a ram to be offered as a burnt offering. There Abraham discovered one of God's identities: *Yahweh-Yireh*, "Yahweh will provide."

This is exactly what God did in the incarnation, by which the Son became fully human. God provided a perfect sacrifice: he entered the totality of our human life. He shared the experiences of work, laughter over family dinner, hunger and thirst, the joy and betrayal of friendship, temptation to sin, and, finally, death itself. God entered the totality of human life and by doing so joined human life to himself forever. Having fully and completely shared our human life, Jesus in his resurrection became our invitation to share the totality of God's life. None of this implies that the cross resolves God's anger and wrath.

The God who revealed himself to Abraham and reveals himself in Jesus is not full of anger. He is not poised to kill us. He is full of love. In his love he provides for us what we are unable to provide for ourselves. He makes sacred every part of our living through the sacrifice of Jesus. This is what we mean when we proclaim Jesus as the perfect, complete, and eternally sufficient sacrifice who reconciles us to God. Not only does he forgive sin, but he frees us to offer prayer and *tzedakah* to God.

Beyond all these sacrificial lambs, there is one other Old Testament lamb that might help us better understand what Jesus came to do and be.

2

Passover

A BROKEN BONE ON the outside of my right hand required a cast. It was quite uncomfortable. The ring and pinkie fingers were wrapped together to keep the bone immobile as it healed. This left a thick piece of cast wedging apart the ring and middle fingers. This space was so wide the fingers outside the cast were as unmovable as the fingers the cast held. Even a yoga master could not have maintained that stretch very long.

I daydreamed how nice it would be to have the cast off so I could reunite my fingers. Finally, the day came. The cast was cut away. With relief, my brain sent instructions to the separated fingers: resume normal position. Nothing happened. My fingers had atrophied into what looked like a permanent Star Trek Vulcan salute. It required several weeks of stretching and exercise to bring my hand back to the condition in which it was designed to operate.

Paul wrote about a similar experience:

> I do not do the good I want, but the evil I do not want is what I do. Now if I do what I do not want, it is no longer I who do it, but sin that dwells within me.
>
> So I find it to be a law that when I want to do what is good, evil lies close at hand.... Wretched man that I am! Who will rescue me from this body of death? Thanks be

Passover

to God through Jesus Christ our Lord! (Romans 7:19-21, 24-25 NRSV)

Paul is describing a spiritual sort of atrophy. His mind and heart deeply wanted to please God. But the forces of habit and personal history nevertheless asserted power over his actions even while he wished they could not.

I confess that part of me feels Paul is letting himself off the hook too easily. Then I recall the number of times I have done something I really did not want to do. Perhaps my words and actions wounded a person I definitely did not want to hurt. I find myself no more able than Paul to actually do the good I desire. Have you ever felt trapped in a sin habit or reaction?

Ironically, Paul boldly wrote just a chapter earlier, "We know that our old self was crucified with [Christ] so that the body of sin might be destroyed, and we might no longer be enslaved to sin" (Romans 6:6 NRSV). He further adds to this encouragement: "Sin will have no dominion over you, since you are not under the law but under grace" (Romans 6:14 NRSV).

The cast is off. We have been set free from slavery to sin, or so Paul writes in one chapter. But in the very next chapter he acknowledges that he is still stuck. It will take years of stretching, moral exercise, and pain to begin working the muscles that had so long been distorted by the pressures of sin: sins we committed and sins committed against us. We are all perpetrators of sin, and we are all victims of sin.

How will Christ and his cross effectively work so we may actively experience the freedom Christ offers? More Old Testament images carried forward into the New Testament may help us find an answer to this question.

During his ministry on earth Jesus lived and practiced religion as a Jew. Part of religious life in first-century Judaism was making pilgrimage to Jerusalem several times a year to participate in several annual religious feasts. These feasts offered opportunity for large crowds to hear Jesus's teaching. Because the crowds came with a shared focus, he became adept at using the feast at hand as a tangible way of helping them grasp what he was saying.

The Passover Mystery

"Is anyone thirsty? If you're thirsty, come to me!" This is a paraphrase of John 7. If you have hung out at church you probably have heard this before. The text informs us that Jesus gave this invitation during the Feast of Tabernacles, an annual feast to remind the Jews of the forty years they spent in the wilderness between leaving Israel and entering the Promised Land. The temporary nature of their long trek through the wilderness prevented them from building permanent homes, requiring them to live in tents or "tabernacles" instead.

As they celebrated this journey centuries after their ancestors had made it, they recalled significant details from its history. Moses led the children of Israel out of slavery in Egypt and into some of the most hostile terrain on earth. The Sinai Peninsula was dry and dead. They may well have felt they had fallen from the frying pan into the fire quite literally. There was no source of food. But they would have died from dehydration more quickly than they would have starved to death. Not only was there nothing to drink, but the arid air quickly sucked any moisture out of their bodies.

There were, by most estimates, about two million people with Moses, roughly the population of the cities of Chicago or Toronto. The few oases along their route would have sustained only a tiny fraction of such a multitude. Their survival was miraculous. God gave them bread from heaven, and when Moses rapped his walking stick against a stone it became a stream of lovely water in the middle of the desert.

In Jerusalem, thirteen hundred years later, Jesus and his people were remembering and celebrating that liminal time of journey. The Feast of Tabernacles lasted eight days. Each day of the feast included a ritual in which all the priests marched in procession from the temple to the Pool of Siloam, a huge cistern at the edge of the city. Each priest carried a large jug, which was filled at the pool and carried in procession back to the temple, where each priest emptied his water jug at the foot of the altar.

The people would follow along with the priests. As they watched they recalled how thirsty their ancestors had been. By the end of this walk, as they watched one priest after another pour

Passover

their jugs, splashing water across the ground, the crowd could not help recalling this great thirst as they themselves had become hot and thirsty walking and standing under the hot Jerusalem sun.

The event recorded in John 7 occurred "on the last day of the festival, the great day," when the crowd had reached its peak. Many in the crowd would have already been through this ceremony every day for a week. The ritual concluded, as always, with a reading from the prophet Isaiah.

> Ho, everyone who thirsts,
>   come to the waters;
> And you that have no money,
>   come, buy and eat!
> Come, buy wine and milk
>   without money and without price.
> Why do you spend your money for that which is not bread,
>   and your labor for that which does not satisfy?
> (Isaiah 55:1–2a NRSV)

Just when everyone was thinking they wouldn't mind having a drink of that water the priest had just poured on the ground, a voice could be heard in the crowd crying out, "Let anyone who is thirsty come to me, and let the one who believes in me drink" (John 7:37–38 NRSV).

Aren't these words a little more powerful when you imagine the context into which they were spoken? Don't they have even greater meaning when you attach them to the history the Jews were celebrating and the thirst they were currently suffering?

Obviously, this wasn't an accident. Jesus had thought carefully about the meaning of the feast, the crowd who would be there, and what they would be feeling and experiencing. He used this all to tie what he wanted to communicate to their history and culture as Jews. This is only one of the times Jesus used a Jewish feast so profoundly.

Our churches regularly repeat a ritual with a purpose similar to that of the Feast of Tabernacles. We repeat a feast within a feast. Jesus and the disciples had gathered for the Feast of Passover. Jesus used this experiential participation in Jewish history by reframing it for us with a meaning inside a meaning. He took bread from the traditional Passover meal, and breaking it, he said, "This is my body."

Reading the Gospels, it is clear that as the conflict between Jesus and the Jewish leaders moved toward its climax, Jesus carefully and intentionally orchestrated his death to take place alongside the Feast of Passover. Of the seven feasts in the Jewish calendar, the two deemed most important were Passover and the Day of Atonement. The holiest place of the temple was only entered once a year, and then only by the high priest. This took place on the Day of Atonement, when numerous sacrifices were offered for the forgiveness of sin: lambs, a bull, two goats, and two rams.

If the death of Jesus were only about forgiving sin, we would have to wonder why Jesus did not orchestrate his arrest and death around that feast and season. Certainly, the Feast of Atonement echoes best the limited understanding of the cross generally taught in Protestant and Roman Catholic churches. What was Jesus suggesting about his own understanding of the cross by arranging to die at the time of Passover?

Passover is the oldest of Jewish feasts. It goes back to when the children of Israel were slaves in Egypt making bricks for the monuments of Pharaoh. God heard their groans of oppression and used Moses to bring about their liberation and exodus from Egyptian slavery.

As the confrontation between Moses and Pharaoh reached its conclusion Moses instructed the Hebrew slaves to prepare a feast. Barbecued lamb was on the menu. There were to be no leftovers: just enough lamb for everyone to eat their fill. If a family was too small to consume an entire lamb, they were to invite friends or neighbors to share their meal so that everything would be eaten with nothing wasted.

When they butchered the lamb for supper, they were to smear blood on the doorposts of their houses. The angel of death was to pass through Egypt that night, taking every firstborn son. But death would pass over any home with bloodstained doorposts. The children of Israel were to eat this meal standing, wearing coats and walking shoes. For when the Egyptians woke the next morning, filled with grief and horror at the loss of their sons, Pharaoh's will to keep Hebrew slaves would be broken, and the Hebrew people needed to be ready to get up and go quickly when the moment came.

The Passover lamb has a completely different meaning from the animals sacrificed on the Day of Atonement. There is nothing about the lamb serving as substitute for sinful people in Passover. Instead, the lamb itself provides nourishment for God's people, allowing them to begin their journey toward freedom and sustaining them on their way.

The blood smeared on the doorposts of Passover identifies people obedient to God. The Passover lamb does not stand in the place of sinful Israel but represents obedient Israel on the way to new life in a new community governed by the law of God rather than an oppressive slave-master.

Look at the cross through the lens of Passover rather than through the lens of the Day of Atonement. On one side we see the Roman Empire, pushed by corrupt Jewish leaders to execute an innocent person. On the other side we see Jesus of Nazareth. Throughout his career, Jesus consistently did several indicative things. He healed the sick. He cast dark forces out of people who had been enslaved to self-destructive and antisocial behavior.

He also forgave sins. This forgiveness reached its deepest level when, dying on the cross, he asked his Father to forgive the very people who had placed him there. We remember this forgiveness in our own reenactment of Passover—the Passover within the Passover—when we lift a cup and quote Jesus saying, "This is my blood, poured out for the forgiveness of sins."

Jesus actively tried to avoid becoming embroiled in the political unrest of occupied Judea and Galilee. When those trying to trap him asked clever questions about Caesar so they could then report to the authorities, Jesus gave even more clever responses, evading their traps. When the people wanted to make him their Jewish king, he simply and firmly refused. He attached himself to the promises of prophets who preached that freedom and restoration would only come through the forgiveness of sin. For as long as the Jewish remnant were slaves to sin, Rome was irrelevant. They were still slaves to their own disobedience.

In the face of plots and threats from the very people who should have accepted and believed him, Jesus remained a perfectly obedient Israel. He was the faithful servant God sought from the time he called Abraham to become a blessing to all peoples and nations.

The obedience of Jesus was resolute enough to accept even the most brutal and humiliating death the civil and religious leaders could impose. Under the pressure of all the violence, insult, and hatred heaped on him while he hung on the cross, Jesus still acted out the love, mercy, and righteousness of God. "Father, forgive them. They really don't understand what they are doing."

In his death Jesus revealed all the dark and destructive power of sin. The cross depicts in gory detail where people, religion, nations, communities, economies—all the structures of human society and life—end up when we live under sin's sway.

From the very beginning God has placed a constant choice before the human race: life or death, obedience or disobedience. Finally, in the person of Jesus a human consistently and fully chose obedience and life. In his final and ultimate act of obedience, Jesus revealed how powerless the "powers" of earth really are. The powers did to Jesus their very worst. In the face of our very worst Jesus retained nothing but our very best.

As the empty tomb on Easter proves, obedience can take the very worst that sin can do to us and turn it around into something redeeming and wonderful. The willing obedience of Jesus broke the power of sin and death. In the same way as the blood of the Passover lamb marked those who were willing to obey and caused death to pass over them, the obedient blood of Jesus freed him and us from the power of sin and death.

Jesus is the ultimate answer to Isaac's question, "But where is the lamb?" He is the Passover Lamb of God who takes away the sins of the world.

Passover

Just as Passover broke the power of Pharaoh over the Hebrew people, the Passover of the cross breaks the power of Rome and Jerusalem. And it breaks the power of Washington, DC, Moscow, Beijing, Ottawa, and all other powers that be. More importantly, the Passover cross breaks such power by ending the deeper spiritual slavery that has kept the human race moving in such self-destructive ways. The obedience of Jesus to love us in the face of our greatest evils has defeated the satanic power that wants nothing more than to kill and destroy us.

The Jewish Passover Feast observed by Jesus and his friends, like the Feast of Tabernacles, lasted for a week. It was also known as the Feast of Unleavened Bread. Traveling on foot quickly does not allow carrying a lot of bread. Bread doesn't pack well. So before making their escape from Egypt, the Hebrews of the original Passover were instructed to bake unleavened bread.

To memorialize this, it became tradition that, one week before the Passover meal, every member of a Jewish family would help go through the entire house, removing every grain of yeast and every crumb of anything that contained yeast. That, of course, would include any sour dough or yogurt that could be used to start the next batch.

When the eight days of Passover were complete, the cook would need to acquire an entirely new batch of yeast. Yogurt and sourdough had to be restarted from scratch. The obedience of Passover requires and offers opportunity for new beginnings. Paul, who had such a personal struggle with sin, also recognized the reality of a new life through the cross: "From now on, therefore, we regard no one from a human point of view. . . . If anyone is in Christ, there is a new creation: everything old has passed away; see, everything is new!" (2 Corinthians 5:16–17 NRSV).

When we regard the cross through the lens of Passover, we see that Jesus has gone well beyond merely forgiving our sin, though that would certainly be gift enough. He has set us free from the power of sin. Slavery is broken, and we are released to walk into a new way of life empowered to live for God and each other in obedient love, willing even to suffer for love's sake if such is required.

To which we all likely respond, "Oh, but you don't know me! I am with Paul in the seventh chapter of Romans on this one. I just get stuck in habits, behaviors, words, and thoughts I don't want but can't seem to avoid or control."

Maybe I don't know you. But I certainly know me. And I know very well the times I've been almost too embarrassed to go back and ask God one more time for forgiveness for the same stupid thing. It can feel like I'm going in circles.

It sometimes seems a lot easier to simply yield to defeat. I find it helpful in those times to remember that Passover fully accomplished the children of Israel's freedom from Pharaoh, but that didn't stop him from chasing them. Nor did it stop them from sometimes wanting to go back to Egypt when they remembered the leeks and onions they had enjoyed dining on by the Nile.

In fact, although they were completely free to start a new life in the Promised Land, they spent an entire generation wandering around the wilderness before they got where they wanted to go. And here we are: free, but still wandering in the wilderness. And angry at ourselves. At least, I am angry at myself when I find I have once again fallen into a sinful pattern I have prayed about, been forgiven for, and promised myself and God I would never repeat.

I don't enjoy being angry at myself. In fact, I find anger generally is an unpleasant emotion. My chest tightens. Anger demands my attention when I want to be thinking about other, more enjoyable things. When we are angry at ourselves for the stupid things we've done and keep on doing, that is our version of wandering around the desert.

Here is the good news: if we were still slaves to sin we wouldn't be angry with ourselves, at least in the same way. As slaves to sin, we're pretty sure it is someone else's fault. Or that its okay. Slaves to sin certainly wouldn't expect any better of themselves. The anger at ourselves when we sin is a wasteland that freed people simply have to walk through. But like the wilderness of exodus, it does come to an end.

This particular self-anger is an expression of our freedom from sin. Jesus set us free, and he also forgave us. So now, the next step of our spiritual journey is to accept that forgiveness and learn how to stop being so angry at ourselves.

Fifty days after the original Passover, Moses climbed Mount Sinai, where he received the tablets of law containing the Ten Commandments. In remembrance, fifty days after each Passover the Jewish people gather again to celebrate all the gifts God has given, but especially God's giving of the law to Moses. This feast is called *Shavuot*, the Feast of Weeks, or simply Pentecost.

For generations Hebrews had lived as slaves, unable to govern themselves or exercise agency in their own decisions. They did not know how to govern themselves as a community. The law of Moses provided them the direction needed to learn to live as a free and responsible people.

Its provisions ensured that, rather than following the examples of nations around them, they could become a community for God in the world, enshrining in their culture and politic an alternative to the coercion, power, and violence of the empires and nations around them. Moses's law was an important tool in finding the newness of life waiting to be experienced in the Promised Land.

Fast-forward a number of centuries and, fifty days after Jesus ate the Passover with his friends, crowds were gathering again in Jerusalem for the next feast on their calendar: the Feast of Pentecost. Jesus, of course, was not there. He had been executed on a cross. But his friends were still there, still in an upper room, albeit now in hiding for fear that they too might be rounded up, jailed, or executed.

> When the day of Pentecost had come, they were all together in one place. And suddenly from heaven there came a sound like the rush of a violent wind, and it filled the entire house where they were sitting. Divided tongues of fire appeared among them, and a tongue rested on each of them. All of them were filled with the Holy Spirit and began to speak in other languages, as the Spirit gave them ability.
>
> Now there were devout Jews from every nation under heaven living in Jerusalem. And at this sound the

crowd gathered and was bewildered, because each one of them heard them speaking in the native language of each. (Acts 2:1–6 NRSV)

Just as Moses's law provided a means to create a new kind of community where God's people could live in obedience to God with love and respect for one another, the new Pentecost gave the frightened disciples of Jesus a new opportunity to create another new kind of community that would be obedient to the original mandate given to Abraham to be a blessing to all nations. The Holy Spirit is the gift that allows us to begin living in the freedom accomplished by the cross.

Like my sore hand, newly freed from its cast, the first followers of Jesus required exercise of the Holy Spirit to begin retraining them into the freedom from sin and servanthood to righteousness that generates a new creation. To value the cross without Pentecost is to rely on the "cheap grace" described by Dietrich Bonhoeffer.[1]

The Holy Spirit leads and empowers us. The gift of tongues was not given as a recreational activity for believers to prove to each other the depth of their spirituality. The gift was given to complete God's mission already in process throughout all nations. Sin is not only forgiven in us; the sin in us is overpowered.

A little more than a century after Jesus died, Melito, a preacher in Sardis (in modern-day Turkey), gave a sermon he titled "On the Pascha." This is the first known reference to what is known as the paschal mystery. This idea has been held continuously since then, though often neglected in some traditions. It remains an important part of Roman Catholic, Eastern Rite, and Episcopal liturgies.

"Paschal" comes from the root Hebrew word we translate as "pass over," so the paschal mystery is simply the Passover mystery. The word "mystery" in early Greek thought, and by extension early Christian thought, does not refer to a puzzle to be solved but to a puzzle that can only be understood by divine revelation. The paschal mystery is a concept that will keep reappearing in the

---

1. Bonhoeffer, *Cost of Discipleship*.

following chapters. From this point I will refer to it simply as the Passover mystery.

Though often ignored by Protestants, I find it a very helpful way of thinking about atonement: how we become reconciled with God. The Passover mystery incorporates four elements in the life of Jesus: his life, death, resurrection, and ascension into heaven. Atonement is the product of the fullness of these events woven together. We cannot understand the cross apart from how it is part of this wider appearance of Christ. The mystery is how the cross is more than the death of Jesus. The difference between the body of Jesus dying on a cross and all the other human bodies that died on Roman crosses is the other events Jesus's body experienced in the Passover mystery.

Jesus, living as a human body, demonstrated by his life along with his words the truth of what God is. This same body, born in Bethlehem, carried the violence of our sin on the cross. In the resurrection of this same body again, Christ defeated death, evil, and destruction. He then bodily ascended into heaven. The ascension was the first time a human being entered heaven to sit with God. God then sent the Spirit on Pentecost, so God could be joined to humanity in the same way the life of Jesus joined humanity to God.

These events combined create a new humanity. Faith is recognizing this new reality.

To repent means literally to change direction: to set a new course. Sometimes, when the weather is just right (or, perhaps, just wrong), my decades-old hand injury still aches. So I stretch it and exercise it, grateful that the cast is no longer there. The Holy Spirit leads and empowers me. But I still mess up, as do you. The forgiveness of Christ is there for when I mess up. Christ is crucified. I need to let my sin go.

God loves us. God forgives us. When, for some reason, we do not exercise our full freedom in Christ, God understands. He knows where we are coming from. He knows that we are victims of sin as well as perpetrators of sin. God understands our failures far better than we do. When we get angry with ourselves and self-defeated, we miss the point of the cross. God has us covered.

3

One New Humanity

I have spent a lot of time, energy, and money studying theology. After five decades of study, I have finally reached a conclusion. The most profound theological truths have been spelled out in children's songs all along.

> Jesus loves me, this I know,
> For the Bible tells me so.
> Little ones to him belong,
> We are weak, but he is strong.[1]

You might use your time more wisely by spending several hours contemplating that song than reading this book. Anthropology, salvation, Christology—it's all there. Another song expounds one of the most important issues in Christian ethics in our time.

> Jesus loves the little children,
> All the children of the world.
> Red and yellow, black and white,
> They are precious in his sight,
> Jesus loves the little children of the world.[2]

I will readily acknowledge the language may not be politically correct. But the message is right on target.

1. Anna Barlett Warner (Public domain).
2. C. Herbert Woolston (public domain).

One New Humanity

The cross of Jesus finds a way to complete every promise from God despite our continuing existence in a world that remains sin-scarred and broken. Sometimes it feels like the world is moving backward rather than forward. After the evils of fascism were so thoroughly revealed in the twentieth century; after so many subsequent advances in international and interracial relations; many of us are stunned and grieved to see a resurrection of dark racial and nationalistic impulses. It is even more shocking to see parts of the church embrace resistance to immigration built on the foundation of religious nationalism.

We may forget that God loves the children of the world, "red and yellow, black and white." But God has not forgotten. We may retreat into a narrow world of national self-interest, but God has not abandoned his mission to create a community uniting all nations and peoples of the world.

It is hard to identify the precise moment when the church of Jesus was mandated to become an international, interracial, and intercultural community. Perhaps it was on the day of Pentecost—the Christian Pentecost within the Jewish Pentecost—when the Holy Spirit sent that first band of believers spilling out into the streets of Jerusalem, boldly proclaiming the mighty things God had done in the native languages of the nationalities represented there celebrating the feast.

Perhaps it began when Jesus sat at a well in Samaria discussing faith with a foreign woman. When the disciples returned from their errand, they didn't know whether to be more shocked that Jesus was talking to one of the hated race of Samaritans or that he was discussing Torah with a female. That was a whole other divide.

Jesus was horrible at observing the boundaries and barriers between people so carefully maintained by religion and polite society. He seems to have ignored categories of race, gender, and even religion. After all, the reason the Jews so hated the Samaritans is that they considered them to practice a bastardized version of Jewish and pagan faith. (In fact, the division goes back to the split of the twelve tribes of Israel into a northern kingdom and a southern kingdom, but that's another story.)

Perhaps the international, interracial character of the church goes all the way back to God's promise to our father Abraham to create from him a people who would bless every people and nation on earth. Perhaps it goes all the way back to a garden where God made male and female equally in his image. It was sin that broke the human race from one another. It is always the work of God to reconcile us not only to God but also to each other.

In the prehistory of the first eleven chapters of Genesis, we read the story of the Tower of Babel. Well after our "very good" creation became warped into more destructive directions, we read about the division of humans into language and culture groups at Babel. It was the start of a confusing babel of collective power struggles, competing national and cultural interests, and a proliferation of tribal gods, each of whom served as mascot and defender of the small collection of people who worshiped at their altar.

The promises God made to Abraham were a response to the divisions that had grown, fracturing the human community. While all other nations of the world were invested in protecting themselves from each other, God gave birth to the Jewish nation as a people who were to serve and bless the world. The children of Abraham were chosen not to remove themselves from others but to be the people who would include everyone. The call to Abraham was the launch of God's intention to bring the nations back together.

Pentecost is a very deliberate reversal of Babel. In Pentecost, the division of language and culture is overwhelmed by the presence and energy of God's dynamic Holy Spirit, who brings people of many nationalities into one human community. As we saw in the previous chapter, Pentecost cannot be understood apart from the cross. Pentecost is the outworking of the Passover mystery: the life, death, resurrection, and ascension of Jesus. The cross makes it possible for humanity to move from the confusion of Babel to the multilingual praise of Pentecost.

So it is not surprising that we find foreigners, outsiders, and diversity around the crucifixion: religious people and condemned thieves, toughened soldiers and grieving women. Weakened by the torture he had already endured, when Jesus stumbled it was a man from Cyrene who helped him carry the cross the rest of the way. Cyrene was where Libya is today. Simon of Cyrene was a dark-skinned Arab. A lot of North American believers get nervous when someone like Simon of Cyrene boards an airplane. Of course the soldiers picked him out of the crowd! Simon is the kind of guy who always gets racially profiled.

The man who forced Simon to help with the cross was yet another foreigner. He was one of group of Roman soldiers overseeing the execution. Watching those events unfold, along with his commanding officer he came to a startling conclusion about Jesus. "Now when the centurion and those with him, who were keeping watch over Jesus, saw the earthquake and what took place, they were terrified and said, 'Truly this man was God's Son!'" (Matthew 27:54 NRSV).

In his letters to churches the apostle Paul explores the theological significance of the cross. Paul, of course, wrote from a Jewish perspective and often linked Christ to the wider history of the Jewish people and God's mission to reconcile the nations to God and to one another.

Paul's inherited worldview, both social and religious, divided the world into two broad categories: Jew and Gentile, "us" and "them." He observed that the distinctive possession of the Jews that prescribed their unique relationship with God was the law given through Moses. Jews believed they had received directly from God what God expects and desires from humanity through the Ten Commandments and the rest of the 613 commandments in the Old Testament, known as the Torah.

Along with Jesus, Paul recognized a tension between Jewish theology in his time and some of the content of Old Testament prophets. The prophets had warned, for example, that their knowledge did not make the Jews special so much as it made them responsible to reveal God to the nations. Nevertheless, repeatedly Paul was called on to defend his mission among Gentiles to other followers of Christ who clung more tenaciously to their Jewish background.

It must have frustrated Paul that some of his Jewish brethren were meticulous about circumcision and a kosher diet but apparently oblivious to what the law required in their treatment of foreigners. "The alien who resides with you shall be a citizen among you; you shall love the alien as yourself, for you were aliens in the land of Egypt: I am the Lord your God" (Leviticus 19:34 NRSV).

Paul argues that the cross renders impossible any barrier between Jew and Gentile. Writing to Gentile Christians in the Turkish city of Ephesus, Paul makes this case:

> Now in Christ Jesus you who were once far off have been brought near by the blood of Christ. For he is our peace; in his flesh he has made both groups into one and has broken down the dividing wall, that is, the hostility between us. He has abolished the law with its commandments and ordinances, that he might create in himself one new humanity in the place of two, thus making peace, and might reconcile both groups to God in one body through the cross, thus putting to death that hostility through it. (Ephesians 2:13–16 NRSV)

Recall that the Passover lamb was not a sacrifice for sin but an act of obedience as prelude to a new beginning. As the Passover Lamb, the crucified Jesus was not a representative of sinful humanity but a representative of obedient humanity. All of Israel was collected in Jesus. As a Jew, Jesus remained consistently obedient to the covenants God made with Israel. He kept the law. He became a light and blessing to the nations. He did all that God hoped for the children of Abraham.

What separated Jews from Gentiles was the Law of Moses. Jews had it. Gentiles did not.

In his body on the cross Jesus completed the law and, in completing it, finished it. The law, along with the mistrust and hostility between Jew and Gentile it generated, was nailed to the cross with Jesus. The cross removed the wall that formed a barrier between Jew and Gentile, "us" and "them."

I love the strength of Paul's language as he describes the death of this hostility. In his death Jesus was able to "create in himself one

One New Humanity

new humanity in place of the two" (Ephesians 2:15 NRSV). One new humanity!

The cross kills hostility. In reconciling all of us to God—everyone!—the cross reconciles all of us to each other. Paul makes this point again and again throughout his letters, and he carries it much further than simply bringing together Jews and Gentiles.

> You have stripped off the old self [the old humanity] with its practices and have clothed yourselves with the new self [the new humanity created by the Passover mystery], which is being renewed in knowledge according to the image of its creator. In that renewal there is no longer Greek and Jew, circumcised and uncircumcised, barbarian, Scythian, slave and free; but Christ is all and in all! (Colossians 3:9–11 NRSV)

The one new humanity in Christ eliminates all kinds of distinctions the old humanity is accustomed to make. The cross supersedes race and nationality: "There is no longer Jew and Greek . . . barbarian or Scythian" (the Scythians were the barbarians who made the other barbarians look genteel). The cross supersedes religious background and tradition: there is no longer "circumcised and uncircumcised." The cross supersedes socioeconomic status and class: there is no longer "slave and free."

Addressing this same principle in his letter to the Galatians, Paul adds gender as one more customary division we are prone to make: "There is no longer . . . male and female; for all of you are one in Christ Jesus" (Galatians 3:28 NRSV). The new humanity reminds us of the garden, where there was but one humanity, in whom male and female equally carried and represented the image and likeness of God.

The differences that have divided us through human history were absorbed into the cross.

These now-obsolete divisions were not natural. They were not part of the created order. These divisions were the product of sin and continuing to live in these divisions is an act of sin. Since the promise to Abraham, God has wanted his servant to be obedient to the mandate to bless all peoples. Jesus's relationships and interactions with Gentiles, women, slaves, and sinners are one of the key means by which Jesus was able to present himself to God as a fully obedient servant. Sadly, the church has been no better than Israel in obeying this vital aspect of God's reconciling work of salvation.

Few of us would acknowledge that we are racist. I think this because most of us genuinely believe we are not. All sorts of racial profiling and judgment are so deeply embedded in our culture they are no more noticeable to us than water is noticeable to a fish. It is only when someone tries to take away the water that fish begin to notice—in a most uncomfortable way. In the same way, it takes some kind of crisis to draw our attention to the prejudices buried in our environment.

Through my decades as a pastor, I noticed there is one situation that can quickly uncover hidden recesses of prejudice and discrimination despite our allegiance to Jesus and the Passover mystery. This moment comes when one of our kids starts dating someone of a different race. Again, simply based on my experience as a pastor, this tends to be a larger crisis when it is our daughter who wants to date outside our group. Like the disciples in Samaria, we manage to add gender to our management of discriminating race and economic class. This said, I have also known parents to meet the new boyfriend or girlfriend without batting an eyelash. I take my hat off to them. They are, in my experience, a distinct minority group themselves.

There is a common view that racism is only a "white" problem. Full disclosure: I am an elderly white guy. Again, basing my thought simply on my pastoral experience I would say that while white people tend to have this problem at a high level, it is not unique to us.

I spent nearly two decades leading a congregation that always had representatives from at least twenty different nationalities. A Sunday never passed without all the major racial groups present in the pews. (Sadly, it took us longer to get that kind of diversity in our staff and boards, but we did finally get there.)

One New Humanity

While it wasn't technically in my job description, I confess I always enjoyed engaging in a certain amount of pastoral matchmaking. I enjoy young love! Once I suggested a particular young man as a potential suitor to a young female congregant. For the record, she and I are not of the same race. She explained that her parents had a hierarchy of whom she could marry and, consequently, whom she could date without her parents going ballistic. The top spot on the list would be a young man of the same race and nationality. This would be the preferrable match. But if she were going to cross any boundaries, the next best option would be a young man of a different nationality but of the same race. That also would be acceptable. Further down the list numbers three, four, and five were each different races described by skin color.

"One step down would be okay," she said, "And I might be able to go two steps down. But after that would be a problem." The young man I was suggesting was more than one step down.

"What if the guy you wanted to marry was a doctor?" I asked.

"That would raise him up a step," she acknowledged. "Maybe half a step for another well-paying profession."

While there was a lot of laughter in this conversation, there nevertheless was a problem I felt I needed to address as her pastor.

"Look," I said, "I'm not telling you to dishonor your parents. But I am telling you that to measure people, including a potential partner, with that kind of classification is wrong. If you are 'in Christ' all that matters is that they are 'in Christ.' And there are a lot more ways to be 'in Christ' than most Christians imagine."

"I get that, but how do I explain it to my parents?"

I advised her to do her best, gently raising the issue with them over time. If she wanted, I offered to go with her to have a conversation with her parents. I had done that before, not to advocate for one suitor or another but to address the issue of race and/or economic difference with parents who were concerned.

I recognize there are many issues that make parents anxious. They worry how such a match would affect their grandchildren's lives. They worry about different expectations related to family and gender among different cultures. These are legitimate worries, but they are the same worries we have regardless whom our kids marry. Every marriage is a blending of two cultures because every family carries a unique culture all its own.

I told my young friend that, as she grew older, she might have to decide whether she valued the way of Jesus and the cross more than she valued the approval of her parents. Jesus never promised it would be easy or pain-free. "Whoever comes to me and does not hate father and mother, wife and children, brothers and sisters, yes, and even life itself, cannot be my disciple. Whoever does not carry the cross and follow me cannot be my disciple" (Luke 14:26–27 NRSV).

I will admit that on those occasions when I have discussed race and dating with parents my words have not been as strong as those of Jesus.

If you think all of this comes easily for me, it might help to know that I grew up in the apartheid of the southern United States and remember the days before racial integration was legally enforced. I know how deeply instinctive internal responses to skin color may be when they have been culturally conditioned into a person's whole experience of life. I know how hard it is to admit to oneself those instinctual responses exist, let alone give them to God again and again until they disappear.

I am the only professional man in the city of Toronto I know to wear cowboy boots at work. There are things in my Southern culture I love and always want to remain part of who I am. I would love to see some elements of my Southern culture continue in my children and grandchildren. But I'm talking about boots and biscuits, not white supremacy and Confederate flags. And when it comes to boots, my children sadly take more after their mother.

I think and hope that racial relations in the town of my childhood have improved in the decades since I left it. But the racism I witnessed as normal and predictable life is certainly one childhood memory I never want my own children to experience. Defending sin in the name of protecting culture is still defending sin. If a culture is sinful, it needs to be left behind, just as Abraham left his home and family, and the disciples of Jesus left their fishing nets behind with their dad still sitting in the boat. We can't change history. But we can change culture. In fact, we can't *not* change culture. It is the nature of history. So when we see elements of our culture rooted in sin, to protect that cultural value and its symbols is to continue in sin.

"In his flesh he has made both groups into one and has broken down the dividing wall, that is, the hostility between us . . . that he might create a new humanity in place of the two, thus making peace" (Ephesians 2:14–15 NRSV). The Passover mystery makes us into a new kind of human. The consequence, Paul continues, is "So then you [Ephesian Gentiles] are no longer strangers and aliens, but you are citizens with the saints and also members of the household of God" (Ephesians 2:19 NRSV).

If you were to see me you would likely think, "He looks like an old white guy." You would be accurate. That is how I look. But the truth is I am not "an old white guy." I am a Jesus guy. I have some good friends who look like they might be black people. But they're not. They're Jesus people. Just like some of my friends who look Asian, or Indigenous, or Middle Eastern, or . . .

It's okay to love the culture we grew up with. If I am "in Christ," if I am truly a Jesus guy, things that are important to Jesus are more important to me than my culture, my nation, my tribe, or my social class. People of Jesus stand outside every human culture saying, "Here is a better way. It is the way of the cross."

It is appropriate to teach our kids how to be good citizens. It is good to pass on our family heritage where the heritage is positive, be it Canadian, American, Chinese, or Italian. But it is much more important to teach our kids how to be faithful disciples of Jesus. That involves introducing them to the beauty and wonder of the diversity present in the new one humanity.

One of my best ministry memories is of a party our church threw for a Syrian refugee family. In 2014, before the Syrian refugee crisis really hit the news, a couple from our congregation were visiting Lebanon. While there they had the opportunity to visit a refugee camp near the border with Syria. When they came back to our church, they reported a massive tent city as far as the eye could see. It wasn't long before the news was filled the stories of refugees fleeing Syria by land and sea, finding danger and resistance wherever they went.

Our church decided to collaborate with a nearby congregation in sponsoring a family coming to Canada. We began raising money to be sure we could help them settle and to provide income for their first year in Toronto, an expensive place to live. By the end of 2016 we were well on the way, with a family consisting of Dad, Mom, a three-year-old daughter, and Dad's brother.

A few months after they arrived, their second baby was born, giving us the opportunity to throw a baby shower for them. As people donated gifts and money, it quickly spread well beyond a baby shower. Mom received a plethora of household and baby supplies. Dad received a book he wanted explaining Canada's history. Dad's brother wanted to learn to play guitar, so an acoustic instrument was purchased for him. And we didn't want to leave the daughter out! She received some clothes and toys, but her favorite gift was a small bicycle with training wheels. Delighted, she was quickly riding her new bicycle around the lounge and front hallway of the church.

As I watched this happy little girl navigate around our lounge, I was struck by how her life had begun in a city of tents and mud, and how different the trajectory this little Muslim girl's life would take in Canada. The Muslim family was overwhelmed by the realization their lives had been changed by a group of Christians half a world away.

As we were raising money and planning, a tide of Islamophobia was also rising across the Western world. Our efforts were criticized by Christian friends who weren't part of our church. I recall one conversation in particular when a friend pointed out that bringing a large number of such people into our country would undermine our own Judeo-Christian history and heritage. It struck me as odd that someone would close their door and their heart to a human family and attribute their actions to Judeo-Christian values!

"But Gene," my friend said, "They're not even Christian! If you are determined to bring someone like that to the country, at least you could surely find a Christian family!"

Jesus lived, died, and rose again for our new Syrian friends just as he died for me. They are not Christian. This isn't a story ending with their dramatic conversion to our faith because of the integrity of good Christian people like us. This is a story of people who have experienced something of the unconditional welcome of God through our unconditional welcome to our city and lives.

There is a long history of conflict between Muslims and Western Christians. That conflict may, to a degree, be traced all the way back to Abraham's two sons: Ishmael and Isaac. But it died on a cross just outside Jerusalem some years ago. It's time those who follow Jesus caught up with it. It's time those who follow Jesus acknowledge the sinfulness of racial and tribal hatreds and root them out of our personal culture as we take up the way of the cross.

4

Forgiveness

On October 2, 2006, a man entered an Amish schoolhouse in Nickel Mines, Pennsylvania, where he shot eight schoolgirls, killing five. The entire Amish community responded by immediately forgiving the shooter and refusing to "think evil" of him. Their willing forgiveness was widely reported in national media.

On June 17, 2015, a white supremacist shot and killed nine African Americans attending a Bible Study at the Emanuel African American Episcopal Methodist Church in Charleston, South Carolina. Two days later, at his first legal hearing, three survivors of the shooting along with five family members of those he killed publicly forgave the shooter, saying they were praying for his soul. Once again, their forgiveness made national news.

Forgiveness is news. It comes as a welcome surprise. Forgiveness is not something we expect to see in this world, where violence is met with anger, hatred, and retaliation. Unconditional forgiveness is newsworthy because it is so revolutionary.

These two stories are only a sampling of similar stories that have appeared in news reports over the years. All such stories that I can recall, without a single exception, share one thing in common. Each person or group of people offering this kind of radical forgiveness attributes their willingness and ability to forgive to their commitment to follow Jesus of Nazareth.

It should be noted that these examples of the unconditional nature of forgiveness do not come without a certain amount of criticism. This is particularly the case in discussion of the Charleston shooting, in which the shooter declared he had no remorse for what he had done.

According to critics, forgiveness short-circuits justice. Some argue that when wrong is done, justice needs to be served, and the quick willingness of victims to forgive ultimately threatens social safety and order and hinders the march toward wider social justice. Others argue that true forgiveness is not possible unless the perpetrator of wrong expresses remorse and actively seeks forgiveness.

We return to the cross. Blood flows from nails piercing Jesus's hands and feet. The blood on his face and back from the torture he endured in Pilate's courtyard is already becoming scabbed and crusty. In agony Jesus looks over at those who have crucified him and continue to mock him. "Father," he prays out loud, "forgive them; for they do not know what they are doing."

We read this in Luke 23:34. Or do we? Most of us are more inclined to remember what he have heard about the Bible or what we have read in the past than we are to actually sit down and read the Bible now. One of the major problems we find when actually reading the Scripture instead of relying on memory is that with each reading we risk noticing something that had never come to our attention before. I am occasionally persuaded that Bible gremlins sneak in at night to mess with my mind by subtly changing what is printed in the text.

I had preached about and quoted this text from the Gospel of Luke for many years. If you are wondering where this is going, you might want to pause, open your Bible to Luke 23:34, and see whether you notice it before I point it out.

After confidently repeating this prayer from the cross for years, I finally noticed a footnote in the text. When I checked the note at the bottom of the page in the Bible I read, "Other ancient authorities lack the sentence, 'Then Jesus . . . what they are doing.'"[1]

---

1. Footnote to Luke 23:34 NRSV.

This footnote requires some understanding of how we got the beautifully leatherbound book we call the Bible. The Bible is made up of many documents written over many centuries. The original documents, none of which are available to us today, were copied and circulated in ever-widening circles so they could be available to as many people as possible. While these documents were copied meticulously, we have to recognize that the people doing at least the first few generations of copies had no idea they were copying something we would call the Bible and treat as sacred text, let alone take as literally as some readers now take it.

Among many documents circulating within Jewish and Christian communities, there were quite a few that are not included in the collection we call the Bible. Over time, faith leaders had to clarify which writings carried the evidence of divine inspiration and which, though important to faith and life, should not carry the same weight of authority. The documents they eventually agreed held special inspiration and authority we call the canon of the Bible.

Scholars indicate that the canon of the Old Testament, as recognized by Protestants today, was in place sometime within two centuries on either side of when Jesus lived. Christians have, for the most part, accepted the Old Testament canon as Jews defined it. We know with more precision that the canon of the New Testament was broadly identified about 250 years after the documents contained within it began to circulate.

In the meantime, all these documents were being copied by hand. By comparing the large number of ancient copies we have we can tell that there are small variations in different copies. If a word were accidentally missed in one copy, that word would then be missing from all copies made from that one copy, and all the copies made from the next generation of copies, and so on. By the same token, if someone wrote a note to themselves in one copy and the next scribe thought it was meant to be part of the text itself, that addition would be present in all the copies in the tree in which the first variation was made.

Forgiveness

While this sounds like it resulted in chaos, the care taken with these copies resulted in variations that are mostly minor and unimportant to the meaning of the text. By having a large number of documents to compare, it is relatively easy to trace things back and determine how the original text most likely read.

Comparing copies of the Gospel of Luke, we know that roughly half the oldest copies contain Jesus's prayer that his tormentors be forgiven, while the other half do not contain it. Alongside the copies we have of the Gospel itself, we also have the text of numerous sermons from very early in church history. We know this prayer was mentioned often in these sermons and was clearly part of the early tradition of Jesus's life. Further, we read in Luke's other contribution to the Bible, the book of Acts, that Stephen prayed almost word for word the same prayer in a text that is not disputed.

Usually, in a case like this, the options are simply that either it was part of the original text or it was added later. But this verse is not usual. There is quite a bit of evidence that this verse was in the original manuscript of Luke. But by the end of the first century, there were a growing number of people who thought this prayer for forgiveness was something Jesus simply would not, and should not, ask of God.

At this time Christians were themselves facing brutal persecution. Roman soldiers, like those who executed Jesus, were still actively torturing and killing Christians wherever they could find them. People who had lost family and friends to the violence of the empire could not accept that God would unconditionally forgive their own tormentors and consequently could not believe Jesus would actually pray for such forgiveness for those who tormented him. Believing this verse to be inauthentic, they removed it from the text of Luke's Gospel.

One scholar, Geza Vermes, argues that, as equally as the texts are divided, whether or not Jesus would have forgiven his tormentors must have been a subject of debate in the second century.[2] It should be noted that the arguments for and against the inclusion

---

2. Vermes, *Authentic Gospel of Jesus*, 231–32.

of this verse were not centered on which was the most accurate rendering of the original text, but whether it was conceivable that Jesus should forgive his enemies when they showed no repentance for their violence against him. People wondered, even if Jesus prayed for their forgiveness, was it possible for God to forgive sin that was not repented? Even if human Jesus would pray such a prayer, they reasoned, he would know better than to ask God to do what God's own justice forbade.

Gradually the broader message of the Gospels seems to have confirmed rather than disproved the validity of this verse. Consequently, after a short time it came to be widely recognized as authentic and was reinserted into the text. Who would have thought such a simple verse could be so complex?

Forgiveness is complex. And it is as controversial today as it has ever been. We see this in critical responses to the quickness of Jesus's followers to forgive those who violently have taken a loved one from them. Can what is not repented actually be forgiven? That is a huge question. It touches on God's response to every person who has not consciously repented sin. It may be worth taking some time to ponder your own response. Can there be true and complete forgiveness where there is no repentance?

While pondering this, we ought to take a related story Jesus told into consideration. Just a few chapters earlier in the same Gospel of Luke, Jesus describes a man who leased his land to tenant farmers. When it came time for them to send his share of the crop in exchange for use of the land, they reneged on their agreement and refused to pay. The landowner sent servants to the farmers in an effort to resolve the dispute. The tenants responded by attacking and injuring the owner's emissaries.

> Then the owner of the vineyard said, "What shall I do? I will send my beloved son; perhaps they will respect him." But when the tenants saw him, they discussed it among themselves and said, "This is the heir; let us kill him so that the inheritance may be ours." So they threw him out of the vineyard and killed him. What then will the owner of the vineyard do to them? (Luke 20:13–15 NRSV)

Forgiveness

On one hand, this is not a difficult question. If we were reading this story in a newspaper or almost anywhere other than in one of the Gospels about Jesus, we would not only expect the tenant farmers to receive a harsh penalty; we would most likely believe justice and social order would require them to receive severe judgement for such an evil act.

But this is Jesus telling the story, so perhaps it has a different, more gracious outcome. Let's see. "What then will the owner of the vineyard do to them? He will come and destroy those tenants and give the vineyard to others" (Luke 20:15-16 NRSV).

The people listening to this story knew immediately that Jesus was speaking about their history with the prophets God had sent through the years. The vineyard was a common and frequent metaphor for Israel. In suggesting this fictional inheritance would go to others, the original Jewish listeners were aghast at the idea that God might remove from them promises they had inherited from Abraham. "Heaven forbid!" they said (Luke 20:16 NRSV).

Parallels to the crucifixion of Jesus are obvious. First the prophets were killed, then the beloved son. Can we conclude, then, that the story of the cross will end the same way? Will the owner of the vineyard arrive, filled with wrath to mete out a harsh justice for the death of his beloved son?

> But then Jesus turned things upside down as the parable came to a conclusion.
> But he looked at them and said, "What does this text mean:
>
> 'The stone that the builders rejected
> has become the cornerstone'?
>
> Everyone who falls on that stone will be broken to pieces; and it will crush anyone on whom it falls." (Luke 20:17-18 NRSV)

Jesus was making two points. He knew his own people were going to reject him just as they had rejected the prophets before him. His people rejected the prophets because the prophets demanded repentance: that the people of Israel change their ways to better reflect the ways of God.

He was also telling his opponents that there is a cost to ignoring or, worse, extinguishing his message. To live in legalistic, graceless, mutual criticism and condemnation would leave them permanently disabled and crushed. But was that a punishment? Or was it a consequence naturally flowing out of their own decision, in the sense that a child getting hit by a car is not a parental punishment but a natural outcome of the child's disobedience, which is why children are told not to run out into the street in the first place?

The story of the cross can end in one of only two possible ways: there will be justice for those who crucified Jesus, or there will be forgiveness. How would the story of the tenant farmers be different had the beloved son intervened on behalf of his attackers? What if the beloved son asked, as his dying request, that the father forgive those who killed the son?

Of course, we don't expect this to happen. All our human experience leads us to think that the last words of the dying son would be to plead with his father for vengeance and threaten his tormentors with impending wrath. I'm pretty sure that is how I would have responded. So I can understand how people facing the very same tormentors would reject the verse in which the Son pleads with the Father to forgive those who lifted him to die on a cross.

Physical pain was only part of the punishment Romans designed in crucifixion. Crucifixion humiliated entire communities.

Some years ago a woman who belonged to a church near the church I pastored came to me for comfort and prayer. Her son had been sentenced to prison for sexual assault. She was torn apart by love and worry about what her son was going through while filled with shame and anger by what he had done. Despite her terrible pain, she was too embarrassed by the nature of his crime to speak with her own pastor or church about it. She feared it would become a big scandal in a small town.

FORGIVENESS

I was generally careful to discourage people from leaving their own church to attend the church in which I ministered. Nevertheless, this woman ended up attending my church. She could never bring herself to face friends in her former congregation. Frankly, I thought she was being a little silly. I thought her friends would actually gather around her with comfort and support. She thought I was being naive. I guess we'll never know.

There was no sentence more scandalous in the Roman world than death by crucifixion. The cross, reserved only for slaves and political insurgents, was a way not only to humiliate the individual being executed but to underscore how powerless entire people groups were to change the social order. The request Joseph of Arimathea made to bury Jesus was somewhat unusual. Bodies tended to hang on crosses for a long time. Usually, family and friends of the convict were too frightened to ask to take them down. Joseph's wealth likely made him a little more secure asking such a favor from the authorities.

Jesus must have known that he had already caused his mother to endure one scandal through the circumstances of his birth. Mary, of course, was pregnant before she was married—and not by her fiancé. It's hard to imagine that such a disgrace would not leave some mark on his whole family. Now the circumstances of his death would expose them to another scandal. What happened on the cross would be hard to forgive.

The good news of Jesus is that God is more gracious than we are. "If anyone does sin, we have an advocate with the Father, Jesus Christ the righteous; and he is the atoning sacrifice for our sins, and not for ours only but also for the sins of the whole world" (1 John 2:1–2 NRSV). Jesus is exactly the kind of beloved son who would plead with his father on behalf of those who have inflicted even their worst violence and humiliation on him.

What, exactly, is forgiveness? In English, to forgive is to stop feeling resentment for a harm done to us or to renounce claim to a debt owed to us. The word used in the Greek New Testament has a sense of letting go of something. In this context, it means to not attach blame for an action. As we might say to an angry friend, "You have to just let it go. Let it be."

Needless to say, that is hard to do when we are hurt and offended. We are owed justice! We desire retribution not only for our own sake but also because we are all protected when justice is done. Second-century Christians were asking a very good question: Is forgiveness actually a good thing? Or is it socially destructive?

Perhaps we can limit the potential destructiveness of forgiveness by turning it into some sort of exchange. Perhaps someone who has wronged us can rebalance that wrong by giving us something in return. The most common form of return we expect is genuine remorse and any possible restitution. If I take your car without asking and dent the fender, perhaps I can make an exchange with you: I will fix your fender and have your car completely cleaned and detailed because I feel so badly about doing wrong, and you, in turn, will forgive me. This forgiveness, then, is a transaction.

Why then, do we find the word "give" in forgiveness? In the case above, you haven't "given" me your forgiveness. I have bought it. Thinking of the other meaning of the English word, imagine this scenario. I loaned you $50, and you paid it back with a little bit of interest. Upon receiving your complete repayment I declare, "That's great, your loan is now forgiven!" How would you respond? Wouldn't you say, "Wait a minute! That's not right! The loan is repaid! With interest! I have done my part. I have balanced the scales. If you wanted to forgive me, you could have said I don't need to pay you back. But now the debt is paid. Forgiveness has nothing to do with it."

It may be that an even more important question to ask about forgiveness as a transaction is with whom such forgiveness leaves power. If I cannot forgive you until you express remorse and make some kind of restitution, who has the power?

I sometimes wonder how life has worked out for a boy who bullied me when we were in high school. He was big and tough. I was not. I had long hair. He apparently did not like long hair and did not like me for that simple reason. He never wasted an opportunity to threaten and mock me if he had a good audience. I felt weak and humiliated, and there was nothing I could do about it. While it makes no sense, it is not the bully who feels shame but the bullied.

There are many miles and many years between us, but I can't help thinking of him from time to time and wondering how he would feel if he met me now. Would he be embarrassed? Does he regard those encounters as "fun times back in high school"? If he had the chance, would he apologize? Or laugh that I still think about it? Of one thing I'm relatively sure. If he thinks about it at all he doesn't think about it and continue to feel it the way I do.

What especially aggravates me about these memories is that I know quite well that, until I forgive him, he still has power over me, the miles and years between us notwithstanding. I will only be free when I can simply forgive. It has been fifty years already. I think an apology is unlikely to come. Honestly, even if he did apologize, I have developed such a habit of resentment that I'm not sure I could let it go. I can only hope and pray.

Could it be that you or I could have a similar power over God by refusing to repent? I know that I am at least capable of temporary forgiveness when my memories of being bullied come. I know that the older I get the better I get at forgiving this old hurt quickly because holding onto my hurt, anger, and resentment is unpleasant only for me. One of the few things that gives me hope that I can simply forgive is believing that God simply forgives. Without condition.

"In Christ we have redemption through his blood, the forgiveness of our trespasses, according to the riches of his grace that he lavished on us" (Ephesians 1:7–8 NRSV). Grace is freely given. We have forgiveness and grace because of who God is. We have not bought forgiveness with something we have believed, nor purchased our forgiveness with something we have done. Forgiveness of sin is not contingent on us. It is the gift of a God who is much larger than we are.

We return to the fundamental choice God placed before his people between life and death. It began in the garden of Eden, where Adam and Eve could eat from any tree, including the tree of life, with the single exception being the tree of the knowledge of good and evil. They were warned that to taste that fruit would bring death.

> Moses, speaking for God, puts the same choice on the table:
>> I call heaven and earth to witness against you today that I have set before you life and death, blessings and curses. Choose life so that you and your descendants may live, loving the LORD your God, obeying him, and holding fast to him, for that means life to you. (Deuteronomy 30:19–20 NRSV)

Death is not a punishment; it is a consequence. It is not the case that God kills us because we disobey his instructions. God instructs us because he knows what brings us life and fulfillment and what is dangerous and destructive to us.

Deuteronomy 30–31 contains a number of choices the almost-born nation of Israel would face. Some would lead to blessing and life. Others would lead to curse and death. If we trace the history of the children of Israel, we will find them living out each of the choices Moses placed before them, sometimes good choices and sometimes bad choices.

At their best, they obeyed the law of Moses in what Jesus once described as the "weightier matters of the law: justice and mercy and faith" (Matthew 23:23 NRSV). Such matters not only reflect the character and behavior of God; they also create a vibrant and strong society. But in the bad choices made by Israel—the choice to worship foreign deities who were brutal and harsh, the choice to protect the wealth of the wealthy and the power of the powerful while refusing justice to the poor and powerless—these choices weakened and hollowed them out from within.

From this place of weakness Israel was eventually invaded, oppressed, and dispersed among the empires that displaced them. This happened to them not as a punishment but as a direct result of doing the dumb things God told them not to do. Somehow, they remind me of me.

On the cross hung one obedient son. He was the bloodied victim of various people continuing the human habit of making death their choice. As we will explore in more detail later, when Jesus cried out from that cross, "My God, my God, why have you forsaken me?" he was giving voice to oppressed people all over the world who suffer the systems of death that have ruled humanity and continue to rule humanity. As history unfolds, it becomes the sad state of affairs that as soon as any of these victims have power to express their own violence and force, they will almost always become the oppressor.

This is the nature of sin. Sin gives birth to hurt, anger, and hatred in those who are sinned against. This hurt, anger, and hatred lead to new sin. God knows what gives life and what leads to death. Responding to sin with force and violence only begets more sin. The only response that can possibly break the cycle of sin is forgiveness. But who is strong and large enough to make such a response?

Jesus hung on the cross without sin. He was the only truly and fully innocent victim of our evil. He did not hang on the cross as a representative of all sinful humanity to absorb the burning anger of God. He hung on the cross as a fully obedient representative of the human race to reconcile humanity to a loving God and reveal to us the merciful grace of a grieving God.

Praying for our forgiveness, Jesus not only reunited us with God; he also showed us the only way true change ever comes. Change does not come through retribution. Vengeance and retributive justice might change the identity of the oppressor, but they never change the reality of oppression. True change only comes through sacrifice, suffering, and forgiveness. It has always been so, and it will always be so.

There is nothing so threatening to the powers that drain this world of life than people who are willing to suffer and die for what they believe. This is why the Romans were so keen to crucify slaves and insurgents who threatened the imbalance of power. Second-century writer Tertullian, saw this: "The blood of the martyrs is the seed of the church."

Peter, forgiven his betrayal the night of Jesus's arrest, also understood the continuing power of the cross. Writing to Christians enduring persecution for their faith, he says, "Christ also suffered for you, leaving you an example, so that you should follow in his steps. . . . When he was abused, he did not return abuse; when he suffered, he did not threaten; but he entrusted himself to one who judges justly" (1 Peter 2:21, 23 NRSV).

While the church was living the cross, Rome could not stop her. The only way Rome could preserve power in the face of forgiveness was to give the church power rather than letting us continue to suffer and die for Jesus. The cross is not only the means by which we are redeemed; it is also the method by which we ourselves can be redemptive in the world.

On the cross Jesus asked the Father to forgive our participation in the political and religious systems that killed the beloved son. He also showed us our mission: to rescue the world by our willingness to follow him onto the cross.

5

Getting Back on Track

The parsonage we moved into fresh out of school came equipped with a rickety old lawn mower. The engine ran, but the blade was so dull and dinged it pulled more grass than it actually cut. Feeling pretty good about being the man of my first house, I went to the hardware store for a new blade and an adjustable wrench to install it.

Returning to the garage, I tipped the mower on its side, got the wrench on the bolt, heaved, and grunted—and nothing at all happened. I sprayed it with WD-40. No movement. I tried tapping it with a hammer. Still nothing. I found a length of pipe to slide over the wrench handle, adding more leverage. Nada. I stepped on the pipe, balancing against the garage, and jounced on it. The pipe flexed a little bit, but the bolt did not move.

About that time my elderly neighbor strolled over and said, "You know that's a reverse thread, don't you?"

"Pardon?"

"It's a reverse thread. If the thread moved the usual direction, the rotation of the blade and vibrations would loosen it every time you cut the grass, and eventually it would just fall off. So it's threaded the other way."

I flipped the wrench around so I could step on it in the other direction. It took a bit more jouncing. By that time I had tightened it pretty good. But once it got started, the nut screeched itself loose without too much more effort. This is not the only time I have badly frustrated myself by trying to fix something only to find out I was doing it the wrong way, and the very thing I was doing to fix the problem was making it worse.

The Passover mystery rescues us from ourselves. God, as Trinity, fixed a problem we were already trying to fix. Many of us were trying very hard. But we were trying to force the bolt in the wrong direction, and the harder we worked at it, the worse we made it. We never dreamed that humility and vulnerability were the tools needed to be more fully and functionally human.

The record of the crucifixion found in Matthew's Gospel contains some dramatic details not included in other Gospel accounts. As if the simple story of the execution of Jesus were not enough, in Matthew the sun darkens, there is an earthquake, tombs open, and dead people wander around the city like some kind of zombie apocalypse.

All these extraordinary pieces of the story had special symbolic meaning to first-century Jewish readers. It is important to remember that the story of Jesus is always, at heart, a Jewish story. This is particularly the case in the Gospel according to Matthew. He wrote directly to a Jewish audience trying to explain how Jesus fixed a problem Jews were uniquely equipped to understand.

Once again, we have to go all the way back to our shared father, Abraham. Jewish history begins with several promises God made to Abram. God would give him a land. God would make him become the father of a great nation. Through that nation, "all the peoples on earth will be blessed through you" (Genesis 12:3 NIV).

Summarizing the time between when God gave Adam and Eve a good creation and when God gave these promises to Abram, everything we read in the early chapters of the Bible is about the world falling apart and getting further from God. There is little but violence and disobedience in those pages.

In Abraham, God was beginning a rescue mission. He would start by creating a people who would know him, serve him, and bless all nations by doing so. But the project to rescue us from ourselves got off to a slow start. The story line carries us quickly from God promising to give Abraham a family to that extended family building Egyptian monuments as Pharaoh's slaves.

We've already seen the angel of death pass over Hebrew households, their doorframes smeared with the blood of a lamb as God rescued the children of Israel and began to lead them into freedom. There were many signs of God's glory in this rescue, from the evidences Moses presented to the Egyptian court that God wanted the Hebrew slaves freed to the parting of the Red Sea, saving them from Pharaoh's chariots.

God's glory first appeared to Moses in the wilderness as a burning bush that was not consumed. Then God's glory appeared to all the children of Israel as the pillar of cloud that led them through the desert by day and the pillar of fire leading them through the night. An even more dramatic cloud of fire appeared on top of Mount Sinai so powerfully and miraculously that no one but Moses dared go near it. In this experience of glory, Moses received the law.

So God's tangible cloud of glory led his nation toward their promise. God would be their God and they would be his people. The law would organize a social and political community that, unlike other empires and nations on their horizon, would be defined by righteousness, mercy, and justice. Israel was to be a unique nation and bless all nations by being a shining example of God's love and righteousness.

But over time the Israelites discovered they didn't actually like being so different. They were like middle-schoolers who want to wear what everyone else is wearing. They were intrigued with the different gods of other nations, who somehow seemed more powerful and fertile than the God who rescued them from Egypt. They enjoyed reading magazine articles about glamorous royal families from other nations and began to wish they had a royal family of their own.

While other people had beautiful temples, the children of Israel still worshiped in a tent patterned after the tabernacle prescribed in the law of Moses that could be moved with them as they traveled across the desert. But now they were settled, it felt like other nations had wonderful gods who lived in cedar temples while they were left with a God who lived in an RV.

God had called them to be an alternative society to the nations of the world. Instead of becoming the blessing to the nations God intended them to be, they simply wanted to be like other nations. So God let them have a king. Then God let them have a temple. But God drew the line at letting them have other gods.

The more the children of Israel sank into idolatry, worshiping brutal and sexualized deities of the nations around them, the more their culture and society shrank into competition for wealth, sex, and power. More and more they got what they wanted: to be just like the nations around them. The integrity and equity of the law were ignored.

As the clout of Hebrew kings grew, the need for prophets to speak for God in the face of autocratic human power grew in tandem. The prophets warned that if Israel continued to follow other gods into idolatrous injustice and violence, the God who rescued them from Egypt would not protect them from the predatory activities of the nations around them. The glory that had kept them safe was finally gone. Their desire to be like other nations caught up with them, and two empires, first Assyria and then Babylon, overwhelmed them and herded them off to actually live with other nations.

Jerusalem, with its magnificent temple and majestic palaces, lay in ruins. The cloud and fire of glory were completely gone: a distant memory for a homesick people. And they got homesick quickly.

> By the rivers of Babylon—
>   there we sat down and there we wept
>   as we remembered Zion [Jerusalem].
> On the willows there
>   we hung up our harps.
> For there our captors
>   asked us for songs,
>   and our tormentors asked for mirth, saying,
> "Sing us one of the songs of Zion!"

Getting Back on Track

> How could we sing the Lord's song
> in a foreign land? (Psalm 137:1-4 NRSV)

To begin with, they had not been singing the Lord's song all that faithfully in their own land. That was precisely what had led them into their weakened state.

But we may want to ask: Was God absent from Babylon? Was God not also present there? The very reason God preferred a tent to a permanent temple was precisely so God could be wherever God's people found themselves. God had revealed himself willing to be a mobile God.

In Babylon, Israel continued in a form of idolatry. It was a trickier, more slippery kind of idolatry, but idolatry nevertheless. Over the years the Jews had turned their land and temple into new idols.[1] They were Jewish idols with some connection to the God of Israel. But they were simply gifts of God. Missing them as much as they did, the Jews were unable to find God in their new location.

Exile in Babylon became a formative experience for what Judaism would become. Among other things, it was a time for collective soul searching. The displaced children of Israel found themselves asking, "How did we get here? What did we do wrong?" In the absence of the temple and the consequent irrelevance of the priesthood of the tribe of Levi, two new institutions appeared: the synagogue and the rabbi.

To this day most Christian Sunday worship rests heavily on the pattern of the synagogue. "Rabbi" simply means "teacher." When Jewish people gathered in the synagogue, a significant element of the gathering was listening to a rabbi explain the Torah. Together the Jews tried to learn from the Scripture where they had turned away from God and how they could be reconciled to him in such a way that his glory would return. They concluded that

---

1. For the sake of simplicity I am using the word "Jew" improperly here. The word "Jew" was first used in the Roman occupation of Judea. When the twelve tribes split into two nations, the northern tribes became known as Israel, while the southern tribes are known by the name of the larger tribe, Judah, from which Judea also was named. The people carried into Babylonian exile were from Judah but would only later be known as "Jews."

strict adherence to the Torah was the key to recovering their obedience to God. They carefully defined exactly what each command required. They were working as hard as they could to remove the bolt so they could fix the lawn mower.

When at least a small number of these exiles were allowed to return to Judah and rebuild Jerusalem, they intensified their effort to loosen the bolt. Their land had not been completely vacant while they were away. They found, in their place, a community of people who came to be called Samaritans.

The Babylonians had not taken everyone. They took those they deemed most capable of leading a nationalistic movement against the empire. But they left behind those who were poor, uneducated, and weak. These people had intermarried with other peoples the Babylonians had displaced from their own lands and moved into Judah.

Not all the children of Israel had accepted the temple in Jerusalem. Before the Assyrian conquest of the northern tribes, the northern Israelites had largely returned to the places of gathering they shared for worship before the temple had been built. (We see this division in the well-known conversation between Jesus and the Samaritan woman at the well.)

When the Jews returned to rebuild, the Samaritans initially were enthusiastic and offered assistance to the returning Jews. One of the first ways the Jews tried to fix their problem with God was to reject Samaritan help, considering Samaritans to be ignorant mongrels. Thus began a centuries-long animosity between the two groups.

A second effort to fix their religious problem was related. All Jewish men who had married non-Jewish wives in Babylon were told to send their wives and children away. Numerous families were torn apart by this effort to be holy.

Both of these decisions are understandable in context. The Jews had come to the conclusion that being like other nations was not at all a good thing. They were repenting of their past decisions. They were determined to remain as isolated from other nations and religions as they possibly could be. They would have no real friendship or connection outside their own people. They built strong walls—of stone and of ideas—to protect themselves from the dangerous influence of other people with dangerous beliefs.

In their quest to restore obedience, they had completely forgotten their initial vocation to bless all the peoples of earth. They forgot the injunctions of the Mosaic law to treat the foreigner and sojourner among them as fellow citizens, remembering that they themselves were once foreigners and sojourners in Egypt. They were working away at a stubborn bolt, but they were trying to turn it in the wrong direction.

A third decision was to rebuild their temple so God would have a place to return to them with the cloud of glory. To their surprise and dismay, when the second temple was completed and dedicated, nothing happened. The glory did not return.

Haggai, one of their prophets at the time, gave those who were disappointed some comfort:

> Who is left among you that saw this house in its former glory? How does it look to you now? Is it not in your sight as nothing? . . . Thus says the LORD of hosts: Once again, in a little while, I will shake the heavens and the earth and the sea and the dry land; and I will shake all the nations, so that the treasure of all nations shall come, and I will fill this house with splendor [glory]. . . . The latter splendor [glory] of this house shall be greater than the former, says the LORD of hosts. (Haggai 2:3, 6–7, 9 NRSV)

The glory had not come, but it eventually would come with even greater glory. One of Haggai's contemporaries, the prophet Zechariah, added detail to this hope.

> Thus says the LORD of hosts: Let your hands be strong—you that have recently been hearing these words from the mouths of the prophets who were present when the foundation was laid for the rebuilding of the temple, the house of the LORD. . . .
>
> Thus says the Lord of hosts: Peoples shall yet come, the inhabitants of many cities; the inhabitants of one city shall go to another, saying, "Come, let us go to entreat the

> favor of the Lord, and to seek the Lord of hosts: I myself am going." Many peoples and strong nations shall come to seek the Lord of hosts in Jerusalem, and to entreat the favor of the Lord. Thus says the Lord of hosts: "In those days ten men from nations of every language shall take hold of a Jew, grasping his garment and saying, 'Let us go with you, for we have heard that God is with you.'"
> (Zechariah 8:9, 20–23 NRSV)

God would return with the fire and cloud of his glory, but the Jewish people waiting to see glory return to the temple needed to know God's glory would only return in the company of the world's nations. Rediscovery of their own Jewish vocation to bless the nations and welcome the foreign sojourner was a prerequisite to the return of divine glory. Either the temple would be a place where everyone on earth could find God, or no one would witness God's glory.

Despite the clarity of Zechariah's message, the Jewish people kept trying to loosen the bolt by doubling down on exclusion. By the time Jesus came several centuries later, the temple and the priests responsible for its operation were a source of considerable debate among the Jews. The Pharisees were critical of its corruption and in theological opposition to its mostly Sadducee priests. The Essenes had given up on the temple and moved to a wilderness retreat at Qumran, where their library would later be found and known as the Dead Sea Scrolls.

King Herod was continuing his father's project of rebuilding the temple in an effort to stake a messianic claim for his family. One of the ways Herod raised money for this project was by selling the position of high priest to the highest bidder. The high priest, Joseph Caiaphas, was recovering this cost by sponsoring and renting booths on the way into the temple. These booths supplied souvenirs and other goods to visitors to the temple. This included exchanging Roman currency, in use everywhere else, for a temple currency that happened to be the only currency accepted by priests. Additionally, animals for sacrifice were sold from convenient pens. A percentage of all these transactions went to the high priest.

GETTING BACK ON TRACK

The most logical place to locate this market was the outer court of the temple, also known as the Court of the Gentiles: the only place in the entire temple complex non-Jews were allowed to be. Even Roman soldiers did not go past the Court of the Gentiles. Although Zechariah said the return of the glory of the Lord would only coincide with the arrival of people from all nations in search of God, the only place people from those nations were even allowed to gather had been taken over for a cheap money grab from Jewish tourists and pilgrims.

For several centuries now the Jewish people had been waiting for the glory of the Lord to return, defining and refining their definitions of the law so they could be obedient and welcome his glory back. For several centuries they had been focusing on exclusion as the path to holiness, doubling down again and again on distancing themselves from the very nations they had been called to bless. They had worked and worked on that bolt. But the glory of the Lord had not returned.

It may not have concerned the priest, Caiaphas, that Gentiles had lost their space in the temple, but it was a great concern to Jesus. In a confrontation that seems almost out of character for Jesus, in the Court of the Gentiles he began overturning tables, spilling the coins of the moneychangers across the stone floor. He had woven for himself a whip of cords that he used to forcibly remove people and the animals for sacrifice from the courtyard. "Take these things out of here!" he shouted, "Stop making my Father's house a marketplace!" (John 2:16 NRSV).

> The Jews then said to him, "What sign can you show us for doing this?" Jesus answered them, "Destroy this temple, and in three days I will raise it up." The Jews then said, "This temple has been under construction for forty-six years, and you will raise it up in three days?" But he was speaking of the temple of his body. After he was raised from the dead, his disciples remembered that he had said this. (John 2:18-22 NRSV)

Which finally brings us back to those dramatic, extraordinary events that Matthew reports at the time of Jesus's death: the sun went dark, the earth quaked, tombs burst open, and dead people roamed the city. In Jewish literature each of these occurrences held symbolic significance.

The prophets promised a day of restoration would finally come after a time of difficulty. This restoration would come when God's people returned to God in obedience. The darkness that fell over Jerusalem speaks of God's displeasure. The violence against Jesus collects the violent and unjust disobedience of humanity and Israel. Jesus, meanwhile, representing obedient humanity and Israel, cries out to God, "Why have you forsaken me?"

The earthquake speaks of judgment, but into this judgment comes powerful assurance of forgiveness and reconciliation. We hear Jesus pray for the forgiveness of his tormentors. Further, the earthquake of judgment rips open the tapestry door to the holy of holies in the temple: the place Jews believed to be a literal overlap of heaven and earth, a place where God could more fully be found than anywhere else.

For centuries the kings and priests of Israel had tried to tuck God safely away in the depths of the temple. When the obedient servant of God remained faithfully obedient even to the point of death on a cross, God broke loose from the temple, literally blowing off the doors. This not only displays God's accessibility to everyone and God's ability to be known everywhere, even in the heart of Babylon; it also stands as profound judgment on the temple system that had come to actually prevent people from encountering the glory of God.

Finally, leaning on passages from Isaiah and Daniel, Jewish literature at the time of Jesus foresaw resurrection of the dead on the great day of restoration. The dead bodies wandering Jerusalem were a declaration that the day of restoration had come.

Biblical scholars are not in agreement whether Matthew meant these reports to be taken literally. Was the temple curtain literally torn, and were dead people actually roaming the city? Some commentators argue that, had these things really happened, they likely would have been recorded by other Gospel writers—and others—as well. Meanwhile, we know that Matthew was intentionally writing to a Jewish audience familiar with these symbols.

Whether or not these events are to be read with historic literalism is an issue of hermeneutics: how we read and interpret the Bible. But literal or not, their meaning for the cross remains the same. According to the prophets and Jewish writers, the day of restoration would require human obedience met with divine forgiveness.

On the cross Jesus, the human Passover Lamb of God, offered his obedience to the Father. The fully obedient servant of God asked the Father to forgive those who unjustly killed him. Completing the law with this act of obedience, the difference between Jew and Gentile—and all the other differences that divide humanity—was nailed to the cross along with Jesus. The way to God is available to every nation, race, and people on earth. Jesus has offered himself to fulfill the vocation given to Abraham's children.

The risen Jesus told his followers not to go home and disperse but to wait in Jerusalem until the Father had given them the Comforter whom Jesus had spoken to them about before he died. As God had promised Abram he would become a blessing to all peoples, Jesus promised these early followers, "You will receive power when the Holy Spirit has come upon you; and you will be my witnesses in Jerusalem, in all Judea and Samaria, and to the ends of the earth" (Acts 1:8 NRSV). We have already seen how, fifty days later, they were gathered in a room praying during the feast of Pentecost.

Suddenly, the roomed filled with what seemed to be tongues of fire and the sound of a mighty rushing wind. Like the cloud of fire on Mount Sinai or in Solomon's temple on the day it was dedicated, the tangible glory of God had returned to Jerusalem! The Jewish hope had been fulfilled!

The Jewish story was back on track. The wrench turning the bolt the wrong direction had been released and now was turning the bolt in the right direction. God's rescue mission, begun in Abraham, was again moving forward. Thus, this first generation of the church found themselves spilling out into the streets of Jerusalem, announcing the glorious works of God in languages they hadn't even learned to people from nations they hadn't yet visited. But they would visit them. This good news is for all nations.

This is not only the story of the Jewish people, nor only the early church. This is our story. We are—or, at least, we can be—living it now. Peter wrote to the church:

> Like living stones, let yourselves be built into a spiritual house, a holy priesthood, to offer spiritual sacrifices acceptable to God through Jesus Christ. . . . You are a chosen race, a royal priesthood, a holy nation, God's own people, in order that you may proclaim the mighty acts of him who called you out of darkness into his marvelous light. (1 Peter 2:5, 9 NRSV)

The glory of God cannot be separated from God's mission to fix the world. The miraculous abilities flowing at Pentecost were not meant for the spiritual entertainment of disciples. Nor were they given to make the disciples happy and joyous. They were given so the disciples could be a blessing to all the nations gathering in Jerusalem for the feast. They were given to move God's restoration project further ahead. The experience of the Holy Spirit is missional.

A friend of mine told me how his brother, who had been deeply involved in church work, suddenly decided he didn't really believe in it anymore. When asked why, he answered, "We go through the motions, and we've done some good. But I can't actually feel anything real in it. Where is God?"

That is the same question the Jews were faced with when they rebuilt the temple and nothing happened. We can keep the machinery greased. We can do some good here and there. Then we read Paul's description of the free-flowing worship he expected us to experience in which "an unbeliever's" heart would be exposed. Echoing Zechariah's prophecy of the day of restoration, "that person will bow down before God and worship him, declaring 'God is really among you!'" (1 Corinthians 14:25 NRSV).

Coming to us as Jesus was not a great idea that God had after Israel had failed to live up to its vocation to be an obedient servant blessing the nations. God knew before any of this story ever started that he would need to come to earth to teach us how to rediscover the fullness of his likeness and image within us. The story of Israel is also a broader story of humanity. Biblical writers were inspired by the Holy Spirit to honestly record their history and perceptions so future generations could read, reflect, learn, and become more spiritually alert and mature.

The patterns Israel fell into, the mistakes Israel made, are the same patterns and mistakes we will make unless we learn from their experience and how it worked out. After the exile in Babylon, the Jews were convinced they could experience God's glory again if they were only holy enough. They defined holiness as being set apart from everyone else. They believed the more strict and exclusive they became, the closer they would be to God, and God's glory and power would once again fill their religious life.

They were pulling on the wrench with all their might, but they were pulling in the wrong direction. Every time they turned away from a Samaritan, they turned further from their mission and the experience of glory. Every time they bragged they had never eaten with a foreigner, that they would starve rather than eat anything "unclean" with anyone "unclean," they moved further away. Every time they broke friendship with one another because they agreed or disagreed with one rabbi's teaching or another, they lost more of their connection with God.

Sound familiar? God's glory cannot be experienced while we are isolating ourselves from people around us. Jesus prayed for his followers: "I am not asking you to take them out of the world, but I ask you to protect them from the evil one. They do not belong to the world, just as I do not belong to the world. . . . As you have sent me into the world, so I have sent them into the world" (John 17:15–16, 18 NRSV). This short prayer contains three ways of describing the relationship of Jesus's followers to the world: we are to be in the world; we do not belong to the world; we are sent into the world with the same mission, to the same people, and in the same way God sent Jesus.

We need to know how to talk to bartenders (publicans) and sinners. We need to have conversations at water fountains with foreign people who practice other religions. We need to know how to explain ourselves to the religious people who find such relationships on our part shocking and offensive. Knowing that we will not always, or even often, help them actually understand what we are doing, we need to learn how to live for God undeterred by the criticisms of religious people. We need to stop wrapping ourselves in bubble wrap.

But we also need to learn to not belong to the world. We need to live as an alternative community in the presence of the nations. We need to renounce the greed, racism, classism, and national self-interest that characterizes the nations. We need to live lives of personal integrity while welcoming into our hearts and circles people who are still caught in addictive and self-destructive behaviors. To be holy without being exclusive is tough. That's why it is so seldom done.

God's Spirit will come in glory where there is an inclusive welcome among people who live gently as obedient servants to God.

6

Agony

Agony is hard to hear. It is the sound a woman makes when she realizes the husband she has loved for sixty years has slipped into the mystery of death. It is the sound made by the adolescent when their first real love dumps them for someone else. It is the sound made immediately after the snap of bone in the car crash. Agony is always hard to hear.

We don't like to suffer. And we really don't like to be around suffering. Suffering reminds us of some terrible truths. We will get older. We will get injured, and we will get sick. We will die. What is worse, many people we love will die before we do. One way or another, we will suffer the loss of everything we have and everyone we love. It is a great irony. While we dislike thinking such thoughts, we will be more free to be happy if we face these realities and decide to enjoy the moment we are in, despite the probability the future will bring suffering.

It would be easier to believe Jesus makes us happy all the time.

So it can be quite hard, and even shocking, to realize that Jesus himself was not happy all the time. While he knew there was a "joy that was set before him" (Hebrews 12:2 NRSV), he had to endure the cross: the pain and the humiliation. It is very hard to hear his loud cry, "My God, my God, why have you forsaken me?"

This is why some of us perform mental gymnastics to explain his agony away.

These words come from Psalm 22. I don't believe Jesus was quoting this psalm so that after the fact people would read this account and conclude he was fulfilling the Old Testament. He wasn't offering proof of anything but the reality of his own suffering. Rather than quoting the psalm, Jesus was praying it. And he was praying it because he was experiencing it. I would write he was living it, but the truth is, he was dying it.

Two thousand years earlier, a man named Moses saw a bush burning in the desert. Out of these strange flames Moses heard the voice of God. "I have heard the misery of my people who are in Egypt; I have heard their cry on account of their taskmasters. Indeed, I know their sufferings, and I have come down to deliver them" (Exodus 3:7-8 NRSV). God did not see the misery of the children of Israel so much as he heard it. It was the sound of agony.

Roughly thirty years after Jesus died, the apostle Paul wrote about the whole universe moaning. "We know that the whole creation has been groaning in labor pains.... Likewise the Spirit helps us in our weakness; for we do not know how to pray as we ought, but that very Spirit intercedes with sighs too deep for words" (Romans 8:22, 26 NRSV). Often the sound of creation is a song of joy and celebration. Sometimes the song of creation is a deep groan, like a woman giving birth. Without an epidural.

One day I see spring flowers, the ocean, or my grandchildren, and planet Earth appears a beautiful, blessed place. Then I read the news to see what the human race is up to. I see refugees in boats too small for their passengers. I read of teens barely surviving bullying (or not surviving at all), and suddenly my previously beautiful world seems like a dark, Godforsaken place. Ironically, misguided forms of religion are behind much that makes the world feel so forsaken by God.

Many years ago my wife and I had a stillborn daughter. While we were deep in the grief immediately following that loss, three different local news stories reported three different babies who had been abandoned, all within one week. Two were found

Agony

in dumpsters, and the other in the cold stairwell of an open-air parking garage. I paced the center aisle in the church where I was pastor and bitterly demanded of God, "Where are you? Why have you abandoned us!?"

"[Christ] himself bore our sins in his body on the cross" (1 Peter 2:24 NRSV). This is not a metaphorical statement. This is not a declaration that God theologically placed our collective sin on him and punished our sins in his body. This is not an idea nor an intellectual speculation.

The body of Jesus was torn by whips and pierced by nails and thorns. His body was bruised beyond recognition by hard fists. His skeleton was grotesquely distorted by being hung with nails on a cross. The violence of human government and religion wracked his body with pain, injury, and death. "He bore our sins in his body" is quite literal.

His body bore wounds caused by the kind of evil we have all participated in. Perhaps I've only been an onlooker who didn't step in or step up to say, "This is wrong! Stop it!" Perhaps the violence I've seen on the news was disturbing, but ultimately I considered it someone else's problem.

I enjoy comfort and wealth provided by the murder and dislocation of the original people who once lived where I now live. The origins of my comfort and wealth were provided by slave labor on both sides of the Canada/US border. l am part of it. So are you. Jesus, the beloved Son of God, is only one of our many victims.

The body of Jesus was battered by the evil people do to one another, whether the evil of savage systems protecting nations, empires, and religion, or whether the more personal evil of shouted insults and flying fists aimed at the weak and helpless. In his body, Jesus bore all of it on the cross.

But I am also a victim. Not nearly as seriously wounded a victim as many, but I have been a victim nevertheless. I have been bullied. I carry my own wounds. Jesus is one with me there too.

On the Roman cross Jesus felt the abandonment of every Hebrew slave whipped into submission by Egyptian taskmasters demanding the bricks come faster. Jesus felt the helpless abandonment of every Egyptian mother the morning she discovered her firstborn dead in the crib. She looked to whatever god she prayed to and cried, "Why have you forsaken us?"

Jesus experienced the powerlessness and wounds of every bullied student and every Pakistani child trapped in the rubble of a collapsed factory where moments before they had been sewing clothes they could not afford but that we buy at a discounted price. Jesus felt the horror of the virgins with rifles who fought at Vimy Ridge, and he knew the shame of every concentration camp prisoner forced to strip naked in front of the guards.

In his own place of pain, shame, and shock Jesus was caught up in all the suffering of the world. The question he cried out from the cross was not a biblical quotation to score one more point of authenticity, nor was it a theological inquiry. Other than the actual act of dying, this cry might be the most human thing Jesus ever did.

There is only one difference between the cry of Jesus and every other human asking where God is and why he has forsaken us. This time, it was the beloved Son who inhabited the place of human suffering and oppression. It was the beloved son who was beaten beyond recognition. God the Creator, through whom "all things came into being, and without him not one thing came into being" (John 1:3 NRSV), joined creation's groan as the universe labored to birth something new.

Even in the humanity of his anguish, Jesus chose to give himself fully to God. His last prayer before death was, "Father, into your hands I commend my spirit" (Luke 23:46 NRSV). Faith takes strange forms. The day I heard of the third abandoned child while the crib in my own nursery sat empty, all that I had left of my faith was to be angry and perplexed at God. My anger and disappointment with him were strange evidence that someone had planted in my spirit a conviction that things could be better than this and therefore *should* be better than this.

We are shocked to hear that churches are bombed and burned by arsonists: whether the arsonist is a Christian white supremist or a radical Muslim. But why are we so shocked? Isn't this the way it is? The way it has always been? That we groan in suffering is actually evidence that, despite feeling we have been completely forsaken by him, we genuinely hope in God for something better.

What is most difficult to accept for people who do not like to even be around suffering, let alone experience it, is that the cross shows us how God's kingdom comes. The cross shows us where the signs of God's kingdom are most likely to sprout up in the world.

John the Baptist heard of the miracles his cousin Jesus performed and sent two of his own followers to Jesus to ask whether Jesus really was the one they were waiting for.

> Jesus had just then cured many people of diseases, plagues, and evil spirits, and had given sight to many who were blind. And he answered them, "Go and tell John what you have seen and heard: the blind receive their sight, the lame walk, the lepers are cleansed, the deaf hear, the dead are raised, the poor have good news brought to them." (Luke 7:21–22 NRSV)

First-century Jews considered all these activities signs the Messiah would display when Messiah came to set the world right. They also demonstrated God's unity with the poor and suffering.

Remember that the Passover mystery incorporates all of Jesus's time on earth from conception to ascension. In Eastern Christian tradition, beginning with early writers such as Irenaeus, atonement—the process by which we are reunited to God, made one with him—is found in the incarnation. Incarnation describes the appearance of God in humanity. In Mary's womb, Jesus literally brought God into humanity.

It is not that on the cross Jesus reconciled God to humanity because up until then God was too angry to bear to have us in his presence. Rather, on the cross, Jesus reconciled humanity to God. He proved the extent to which God loves and stands with the lame, the blind, and the poor. In his healing ministry Jesus displayed in action the love and concern God has for those who suffer. His healing provided tangible demonstration that suffering is not a punishment for sin but an inevitable universal reality that God cares about.

The Passover Mystery

On the cross, Jesus, recognized even by Roman soldiers as the Son of God, embraced the full depth of human suffering. He embraced the physical suffering of nails and fists. He embraced the equally painful sufferings of shame, confusion, and the dismay of feeling abandoned. Jesus brought human suffering into God. And Jesus brought God into human suffering. He revealed a God who does not stand above our pain but enters into suffering's journey and walks its difficult path with us.

Look at the people standing around the cross. The cross is not Jesus making a human appeal to an angry God. The cross is Jesus expressing divine solidarity with a suffering humanity.

He felt the pain of my stillborn loss. Being one with that pain, he resolved my anger and reconciled me to God. Only through such a Savior as Jesus could I see that my loss was not something God caused but something God was grieving alongside me.

We do not handle suffering well. This should be obvious. It is suffering. Remaining the fully obedient servant of God representing all humanity on the cross, Jesus dealt with his suffering by turning in deep faith even to the God he felt had abandoned him. "Father, into your hands I commend my spirit."

With credible solidarity in suffering he took my hand. With credible obedience in faith he took God's hand. And he rejoined our hands together. This is how the kingdom comes. Only through suffering and faith together can a new world be born.

As I write, bombs and rockets are being exchanged again between Israel and Palestinians in the Gaza Strip. This has happened so often before, and this conflict is so deeply engrained on both sides, that it is hard to believe there could possibly be any kind of new beginning in that region of the world. People in Gaza live every day with incredible hardship, whether there is an active exchange of violence going on or not. Their suffering awakens the world to more mundane daily injustices.

It may be that the only faith we can generate in such a hopeless situation is anger and protest that God allows such things to happen. For many, religious tradition inhibits us from giving expression to that anger and protest. But when we cry, "Why have you forsaken us?" this is the Lord's Prayer just as much as when we pray, "Our Father, who art in heaven . . ."

Setting the cross as our example, we understand that it is human to suffer and that a willingness to suffer in solidarity with others is the path by which social change can come, temporary as it may be in this world. It may be that the best response followers of Jesus could make to suffering in Gaza is to be incarnate in Gaza, that is, to take our own bodies to Gaza, where bombs are falling. To literally stand with those who suffer is to join Jesus on the cross in full knowledge that the present powers in the world will do whatever they can do to protect their self-serving dominion against the force of sacrificial love.

The best way we may be able to fulfill the mission of Christ is to venture ourselves into the darkness of the Godforsaken world and, by our willingness to love and to suffer because we love, show the world in a real way it is not forsaken at all.

Jesus offered his full self, body and spirit, to God in solidarity with us. Now we wait to see what God will do with this willing sacrifice.

7

A New World Begins

Sometimes I think I should meet regularly with a group to whom I introduce myself, "Hi, I'm Gene. I'm addicted to the news." For as long as I remember I have followed the news closely. For many years it was enough to listen to one or two radio or television newscasts a day, read the paper, and subscribe to a news magazine, which I usually read cover to cover within twenty-four hours of its arrival. But as with so many addictions, the internet has made things easier and much, much worse. I can now check multiple news sources half a dozen times a day or more, finding articles from broadcast media and print media all in one place.

Even I, as a hardcore addict, realize what a colossal waste of time this is. Specific events might be reported hour by hour, but the main stories do not change much month by month, let alone week by week or day by day. I suspect that if I recited the main news stories I have read in the last twenty-four hours as I write, at least 80 percent of those stories would be still in the news whenever it happens to be that you are reading this.

Violence in the Middle East is unabated. People of color are harassed by police in numbers considerably greater than their proportion of the population would suggest. Refugees risk their lives fleeing danger and war. A large portion of the population responds to refugees with great concern for the refugees' well-being.

An equally large portion of the population responds with concern that they might come here and mess up our nice lives. The rich get richer. The poor get poorer. Politicians want the best for the nation so long as it is not enshrined in an opponent's plan. Men and women acquire wealth and influence in inequitable measure. Lots of evangelicals don't want transgender people in their bathrooms.

Why do I keep up with this stuff? If ignorance is bliss, I really need to stop paying attention to the news. What a messed-up world we live in!

Like Lucy and her siblings in the wardrobe in *The Lion, the Witch, and the Wardrobe*, there an entirely different world that can open to us. A new realm has begun in which life is governed by a loving God. While it is still true that problems exist, it is also true that, in this other world, people are filled with realistic hope. Despite the complexity of the problems before us, God is in charge.

As the inhabitants of this world give themselves to God and so respond to life and the world in a godly way, problems eventually will be resolved. Every day, people from all races, nations, tribes, and cultures gather to share food and life with each other. No one is excluded except by their refusal to participate.

If our era as reported by news media is a strange time, the good news of the cross makes this an even stranger time. We can inhabit one world, the world of the news broadcast, or we can simultaneously inhabit two very different worlds. We get to choose which of these creations attracts our hearts and attention.

Two unnamed followers of Jesus made this discovery while they were traveling one very sad day. They were discussing events that had dominated the news in their region in the previous few days, during which Jesus had been arrested and executed, and then his body had gone missing. While they were discussing these things, Jesus himself caught up with them on the road and joined their conversation. But they did not recognize him, so as far as they knew he was just a stranger.

He asked what they had been talking about. They were astounded he had not heard the news. They told him in the past few days they had experienced the sort of events that make a person not want to watch the news anymore. They described the kind of injustice that too often happens in this world. They explained how Jesus of Nazareth had been railroaded: "a prophet mighty in deed and word before God and all the people, and how our chief priests and leaders handed him over to be condemned to death and crucified him. But we had hoped that he was the one to redeem Israel" (Luke 24:19–21 NRSV). They thought it impossible that anyone, even a stranger to Judea, could have missed hearing about the execution of Jesus.

I wish this sort of story were not such a common occurrence. The world reported in history books and newscasts repeats the broad outlines of the crucifixion story pretty much continuously and perpetually. Any hint of threat to the powerful is met with retaliation. Despite the blindfold worn by Lady Justice, it seems the rich and powerful stay rich and powerful. Justice is not really required so long as they can make it look like justice.

Canada's official celebration of its 150th birthday in 2017 generated a certain amount of controversy over when and where Canada began. Some advocated a 1604 settlement in what is now Nova Scotia. Others claimed the more permanent settlement of Quebec in 1608. Still others recalled a much earlier Viking settlement in Newfoundland. This debate, however, did nothing to diminish the celebration of 150 years of Canada across the nation.

The party cost $500 million. What we were celebrating, of course, was not the origin of Canada. We were spending half a billion dollars to celebrate how European people came and took an entire continent away from those who had lived here as organized nations for thousands of years.

Newsworthy and historically interesting events seem to happen in similar ways. Someone wins. Someone else loses. Winners write history books. When losers tell their side of the story, winners call it whining. The story these two disciples told Jesus on the road, the story of an unjust execution of a good and innocent man, is simply the way things happen in this world. You can't make an omelet without breaking an egg.

A New World Begins

Meanwhile, there are other things that simply don't happen in this world. As a boy I visited military cemeteries in Normandy, France. Each of the white crosses that seemed to stretch for miles marked the grave of a soldier who stayed dead. Lynching victims don't come back to life. Genocides produce mass graves of people who are gone from this world forever.

But the news shared by the two followers of Jesus ended with a strange twist.

> Some of the women of our group astounded us. They were at the tomb early this morning, and when they did not find his body there, they came back and told us that they had indeed seen a vision of angels who said that he was alive. Some of those who were with us went to the tomb and found it just as the women had said; but they did not see him. (Luke 24:22–24 NRSV)

People have speculated why the two disciples on the road to Emmaus did not immediately recognize Jesus. Some say that it was late afternoon and the sun was in their eyes. I think it is not at all surprising they did not recognize him. We have no frame of reference for recognizing someone we absolutely know to be dead when they catch up with us for a walk.

It is at this point that the story told by these travelers veers away from the news as we usually read it. State and religious authorities murder dangerous people so they will stay dead and stop causing trouble. The possibility of an actual, literal resurrection in which the dead victim becomes alive again simply does not exist in this world. It is scientifically impossible. It is historically unique, at least in the world of news broadcasts.

The man with whom they shared the road replied that all they reported could actually be found in the prophets of the Old Testament. As they discussed the Bible and Jesus, they came to the village in which the two original travelers lived. Night was falling, and they persuaded their fellow traveler to stay the night with them.

They sat down together for dinner. Jesus reached for the loaf of bread. He broke the loaf, handing each of them a piece. "Then their eyes were opened, and they recognized him; and he vanished from their sight" (Luke 24:31 NRSV). This experience not only opened the eyes of these disciples to recognize Jesus himself. Their eyes were now open to the possibility of a new creation born in the death and resurrection of Jesus.

As Jesus prayed for our forgiveness on the cross, teaching us the power of forgiveness in our own hurts and wounds, the cross achieved the final defeat of human slavery to sin. Death had always been the product of sin in the old creation. Beginning with Adam, humanity had failed to be God's obedient servant, nurturing and living in harmony with creation.

When Jesus offered himself as an obedient servant to the point of death at the hands of oppression and injustice, and still did not respond with hatred or violence, it is almost as if death worked backwards. But perhaps it is more accurate to say everything had been going backwards, and in the obedient death of Jesus creation finally began to move forward again. The combined defeat of sin and death opened the way to a whole new world.

Defeating sin and death on the cross, Jesus became, as the apostle Paul phrases it, a "new Adam." He became the start of a new humanity, finding its purpose and identity as an obedient servant to God. As we once inherited sin and death from the first Adam, we now inherit godliness and life from the second Adam.

When followers of Jesus filled the streets with good news declared in many languages on the day of Pentecost, the bystanders very naturally asked, "What does it mean?" Peter answered that though Jesus of Nazareth had come, "attested to you by God with deeds of power, wonders, and signs that God did through him among you, ... you crucified and killed [him]" (Acts 2:22-23 NRSV).

Again, very reasonably, they asked, "What should we do?"

"Repent, and be baptized, every one of you, in the name of Jesus Christ so your sins may be forgiven and you will receive the Holy Spirit" (Acts 2:38 NRSV).

We often equate the word "repentance" with sorrow and remorse for either things we have done that are wrong or good things that we should have done but failed to do. Repentance is not sorrow or remorse, although those emotions quite often provide motivation to repent. The word used by Peter in Acts 2 and by others elsewhere in the New Testament that is translated "repent" means to make a U-turn, to reverse our direction. It implies a change of mind leading to a broader change of action and life.

This is what Peter told the crowd they needed to do if they wished to respond to the death of Jesus at human hands in some manner. A change of direction, of course, presumes awareness there is something wrong with the current path we are following. Executing innocent people leads to further death and destruction. In the memory of the bloody cross, the inhabitants of Jerusalem could clearly see the direction they and their world were headed.

Repentance, Peter continued, is followed by baptism. Following a long-standing Jewish tradition of ritual washing as a symbol of purification, people listening to Peter would have been quite familiar with the ritual baths into which priests immersed themselves before entering the holier areas of the temple. Such baths dotted the city of Jerusalem and are still attached to many synagogues today. John the Baptist had used this symbol with great effect, attaching religious purity to willingness to repent: to replace sinful thoughts and behaviors with good.

In these ritual washings, the Jewish tradition was to completely immerse oneself under water. As early Christians witnessed this ritual, it reminded them of the burial and resurrection of Jesus. When people wanted to redirect their lives to flow with Christ's new creation and participate in a new kind of world, they would be "buried" under water and then "resurrected" as members of the new humanity in Christ. Paul summarized this understanding of Christian baptism: "We have been buried with him by baptism into death, so that, just as Christ was raised from the dead by the glory of the Father, so we too might walk in newness of life" (Romans 6:4 NRSV).

In the Passover mystery, the death of Jesus cannot be separated from his birth, resurrection, and ascension into heaven, and the events of Pentecost. Death and life are intertwined. The new humanity we can experience because of Jesus is made possible by the activity of the Holy Spirit to empower a new way of life from within us.

Peter invited the crowd gathered at Pentecost to choose life. They had seen for themselves how life works in the world, at least that experience of the world we read about in the news. They had long identified with the hatred, tribalism, injustice, and apathy about the less fortunate that so often makes us embarrassed to be human. If they really wanted to respond to the crucifixion of Jesus, they would begin by choosing a different way to be human and a different way to inhabit the world. Only the Holy Spirit of God would give them the ability to live up to this possibility.

This was definitely not business as usual. After Jesus was killed some of his closest friends went back to fishing. It was the only life they had known before he arrived on the scene. But once they realized Jesus had risen from the dead, they could not go back to what they had once been.

The birth of a new humanity requires the old humanity in us to die. A resurrection requires a burial. Baptism is a symbolic way of declaring that our part in the world as it is must die. Paul describes a new perspective brought about by the knowledge that Christ died for all of us: "From now on, therefore, we regard no one from a human point of view. . . . If anyone is in Christ, there is a new creation: everything old has passed away; see, everything has become new!" (2 Corinthians 5:16–17 NRSV).

We find a new way of seeing people around us. The old divisions and classifications have become irrelevant. We find new ways of solving problems. We can see plainly that the old recourse to coercion, violence, or injustice simply doesn't work for the long-term common good. We must find new ways to be families and to be friends. We must find new ways to be nations and cities. This new perspective is rooted in the life and teaching of Jesus, which is further inspired in us by the Holy Spirit. We learn to love enemies, to pray for persecutors, to give without expecting to receive anything in return. The new world looks a lot like the Sermon on the Mount.

A New World Begins

Indeed, it takes a new kind of human to be happy when we grieve or because we are being persecuted for the sake of what is actually good and right. These make no sense at all in the old way of seeing things. But through the eyes of a new creation, they become a way to live with hope, joy, and love no matter what the old creation may bring us.

To trust the cross and follow Jesus into resurrection requires willingness to embrace values that are initially countercultural and counterintuitive. Faith is what we call this willingness to embrace what is not only different but culturally difficult. The way of Jesus is generally not a way to success, prosperity, and acclaim.

Evangelists who promise that believing in Jesus will make us rich and happy only make such promises because they themselves continue to see the world through the eyes of the old creation. It would be a serious mistake to think all people or churches that call themselves Christian are actually actively participating in the new world Christ offers. In fact, many religious movements are popular, prosperous, and powerful precisely because they package new promises in Christ with old ways of getting ahead in the world.

While the empire that crucified Jesus knew you had to break a few eggs to make an omelet, Jesus and his followers know that we will be broken. And if eggs get broken, at least an omelet can be resurrected out of the mess. Sometimes the way of Jesus ends at a cross. As Jesus pointed out to his followers shortly before his execution, "If the world hates you, be aware that it hated me before it hated you.... If they persecuted me, they will persecute you" (John 15:18, 20 NRSV). On the other hand, "Woe to you when all speak well of you, for that is what their ancestors did to the false prophets" (Luke 6:26 NRSV).

It requires faith to actually live with such values. In faith, even death on a cross is good news. Death on a cross publicly declares that not everyone has given in to the powers that oppress and coerce. Not everyone has sold themselves to the belief that the one who dies with the most toys wins. Not everyone has given up on love and the common good and those other values that distress the competitive empires of the world. The cross is good news even before the resurrection.

When we know that our cross, like the cross of Jesus, also comes with a resurrection, this is good news indeed. This is why we willingly bury ourselves in the water of baptism in living hope that a new life in a new world lies ahead. Each person who follows Jesus to their own cross, whatever form of loss or suffering that cross might take, makes the love and rule of God more visible in the world.

When Nazis overran Holland during World War II, as in other places ruled by the Third Reich, Jews were forced to wear a yellow star to identify themselves as Jewish. What was different in Holland was the number of Christians who were willing to also wear the yellow star, making it impossible for the Nazis to actually identify by that mark who was Jewish and who was not. This was a dangerous and courageous act by many people. Faith is that kind of courage. "I may die. But I won't give up on love, the common good, and a belief that out of my death a new world might be born."

To stand for Jesus and the cross is to stand not only *for* the oppressed of the world but *with* the oppressed of the world. Somehow you and I need to bring faith's courageous way of seeing things into every aspect of our lives. How would life be different if we brought such faith into our relationships with in-laws? With our irritating neighbor? With our spouse or friend when we are angry at them? With our fiercest competitor in the workplace? With the bully at school?

God's new world is birthed by many crosses followed by many empty tombs on the day of resurrection. Jesus made it possible for us to learn the depths of freedom that come with forgiveness. Jesus made it possible to begin experiencing newness of life here and now.

We live in interesting times. The old creation has not fully passed away. But acknowledging the continuation of the old creation can be a cop-out. We can use that realization as an excuse to let the world suffer because it will all be well when Christ comes again. There is far more I do not know than what I do know about how and when Christ will come again. But there must be at least a possibility that deferring our obedience to the mission of God in the world somehow also defers his return and the final renewal of the universe.

The world is somewhere between midnight and dawn. A new day has begun, but the dawn at which it will be evident to everyone still lies before us. Believing in the cross and the empty tomb, we know it is already the new day. We feel it in our bones and begin to live it with each other. We just don't know the exact time. It may be 2 a.m., or 4 a.m., or 6 a.m. But we know that a great dawning is coming.

On that great dawn, the same Jesus who suffered, died, was buried, and on the third day rose again to ascend into heaven, that same Jesus will return bringing all of heaven with him. Nothing of the pain and harm of the old creation will survive the fullness of his love. His love will overwhelm every darkness and hatred. What a celebration that will be!

The message of the Bible is not about how we can be good so we can go to heaven. The message of the Bible is about God being good enough to bring heaven to us. This only happens as God's goodness begins to emerge in us.

Two discouraged disciples made their way to the town of Emmaus. Later that night, two invigorated disciples returned to Jerusalem with a new message for their friends. Their understanding of the world and how it works had been shattered by the Passover mystery of Jesus. Death and resurrection had launched a new humanity, occupying a whole new world. Everyone needed to know the great change had begun.

8

The Gospel

In 1970, at the age of sixteen, I somehow found myself in the back pew of Wesley Heights Methodist Church, a small congregation in the town where I grew up. I could have counted the times I had been in a Protestant service on one hand. With fingers left over.

On the platform a group of young people, many of whom I knew from high school, were singing about God and Jesus. About midway through the songs a girl from my homeroom class sang a solo called "I Believe God Is Real." I really don't know why it affected me the way it did, but as she sang, I could feel something stirring inside me.

I had only attended church that morning because one of my best friends had joined the youth choir and invited me to come hear them. I was there for Mike, not God. I wasn't particularly searching for God. I wasn't even particularly interested in God. But as that girl sang about how she experienced the reality of God, I found myself bowing my head and praying the first sincere prayer I had prayed in many years, if ever: "God, I don't know if you even exist. But if you do, I need help."

As the church service wound to its conclusion, the group announced they would finish with a final song. It was a slow, heartfelt ballad about coming to God just as we are. But I stopped paying attention to the words early into the tune because, shortly into the first verse, I saw a girl walk quickly up the center aisle. She was clearly emotional, obviously crying. The pastor moved toward her and stood speaking gently with her for a moment. Then they both knelt at a front pew.

This was quite puzzling to me. Considering the situation, I speculated she had somehow just learned of the death of a person quite close to her. For some reason, perhaps the intensity of the scene, I imagined it was her father who possibly had died. The pastor, obviously, had also received this sad news and was now comforting her.

As I was coming to this conclusion, another girl, about the same age, did the same thing. This fit quite neatly into the narrative I had created. Obviously, this other girl was close friends with the first (in fact, it turned out that she was) and had just been told why her friend was in such a state, so she had gone up to comfort and grieve with her bereaved friend.

But then, from my vantage point in the back pew, I saw several more people leave their seats and walk toward the front of the small church. My narrative was beginning to fall apart. It was the last song, after all. Couldn't these people just wait for the end of the service to comfort each other? I began to search for another explanation for what I was seeing.

I happened to be in a seat at the end of the pew. Next to me to the left was a small elderly woman. The top of her head came about to my shoulder. To the right was nothing but an empty aisle. I turned and asked the woman standing next to me, "Do you know what is happening up there?"

"They're getting saved!" she said, with a glowing smile.

"What?" I asked.

"They are being born again!"

I found myself wishing I had not taken a seat on the aisle because, if I hadn't, there might have been someone to my right. I could have asked them what was going on. That poor old lady was clearly more confused than I! She was speaking English, but she wasn't making any kind of sense. I left the building that morning still completely perplexed by what I had witnessed and experienced.

But I knew something had happened between myself and God. When I arrived at home, my parents asked how the church service had been. The only answer I could give was I thought I had met God. This was the only way I could begin to explain whatever had happened inside me when I had prayed that short prayer.

I said nothing about the commotion at the front. I was still puzzled about it and too distracted by the unusual new feelings in me to give it much thought. And my parents were already struggling to come to terms with the possibility I had found religion.

It was months before I became relatively fluent in the strange language spoken by my elderly neighbor in the back pew. It turned out she wasn't experiencing dementia at all. She was speaking the language of evangelicalism.

As I moved deeper into the culture, I discovered I had not followed the approved procedure for "getting saved." My little prayer for help lacked pretty much all the content people later told me is necessary for salvation.

In time I did learn the correct "sinner's prayer" I apparently should have prayed. I even became adept at talking other people into praying it. It goes something like this: "Lord, I know I'm a sinner. I know Jesus died in my place so I can be forgiven. I trust you and thank you for saving me. I dedicate my life to you."

Even as I taught the proper formula to others, I was aware the sequence of realizations in the "sinner's prayer" was not what happened in me, nor how it felt to me. I didn't think of myself as a sinner. I felt lonely and helpless. But I also felt something in the universe loving me. A lot! In my mind, it had nothing to do with Jesus on the cross dying for my sins. I had no understanding of that, and honestly, it never came close to entering my mind. Whatever happened in me that morning simply had to do with responding to a massive embrace of love in the universe I identified as the thing people call "God."

Over time I studied the Bible and theology and became quite proficient with religious language. I became a pastor, preaching and teaching "the gospel." What I once called "winning souls" continued to be my highest ministry priority, although I stopped using that phrase as I became either too sophisticated or too sensitive to the people I was trying to introduce to Jesus. Eventually I came think "winning souls" is not an appropriate way to describe sharing the good news of Jesus with others. At the end of the day all I really wanted then (and still want now) was to help people experience what I had experienced in such a wonderful and soul-healing way.

I learned many ways of communicating "the gospel." They all followed a similar pattern. All of us have messed up, missed the mark. This makes God very angry, because God is holy and perfect and can't allow anyone who sins to get near him. Fortunately, he loves us so much he sent his Son. Since a God of justice and judgment has to punish someone, he punished Jesus on the cross for our sins.

According to this version of the gospel, satisfied that at least someone had suffered and died as a punishment for sin, God is willing to forgive us. But to do this he requires us to believe in Jesus. If we believe in Jesus, confess our sins in a "sinner's prayer," and tell other people about Jesus, we will be saved. "Saved" means that when we die we will go to heaven instead of going to hell, which is what we actually deserve.

This sequence of realization, prayer, and commitment to Christ is what we called "the gospel." I was taught that people who are truly Christian know and believe this gospel, whereas the many people who don't believe it this way only think they are Christian but aren't truly born again, even if they go to church, pray, and all the rest of it.

It is hard for me to write this without sarcasm or bitterness because this set of beliefs often was damaging to my relationships with friends and family: people whom I deeply love and appreciate. In a lot of ways it wasn't good for my own mental health either. By the time I found myself in Bible college, this understanding of the gospel was already fraying at the edges for me, even as I was learning it more thoroughly.

The Passover Mystery

It never seemed like the explanations of the gospel I was learning were in sync with what I had actually experienced in the back pew of that little Methodist church. What I experienced was unconditional love that had literally transformed and reshaped my entire life.

Because of this dissonance, as I tried to explain the good news of Jesus to nonreligious people, I formed the habit of first prescribing the formula and immediately following it up by describing my own experience. My story about my prayer and the lady in the pew seemed to do a better job of telling people outside the evangelical bubble what it actually feels like to encounter God.

Increasingly, I realized I had always been attracted to a different kind of Jesus from the Jesus most of my evangelical friends talk about. I found the "Troublemaker" in Willie Nelson's song (with his sandals, long hair, and motley friends) to be far more attractive than any Jesus I was likely to see in a stained-glass window.

I was aware that, when I preached about Jesus as one who would revolutionize our small world and upset the apple cart of our nice and orderly religion, it made a lot of people sitting in the pews squirm. Some of them squirmed so severely they eventually wriggled all the way into the pews of other churches! One reason I persisted was a continuing observation that not only did the Troublemaker Jesus draw me, but he was a sage sought by the kind of person I had been before I became a church person.

The older I got, the more I read and studied, the more I thought and prayed, the less the doctrinal foundations of the gospel I had been taught made sense to me. When I read Scripture or entered deeply into prayer, the God I encountered did not seem nearly as angry as the God pictured in gospel booklets. That God was depicted seated on a throne, a large flaming chasm of sin separating heaven from humanity. Meanwhile, God continued to meet me as God met me in that church service may years before: as complete, absolute, and unconditional love.

I wondered, if God wanted to forgive us, why couldn't God just forgive us? If someone is punished and pays the price, can that really be called forgiveness, or is it merely accepting payment of a

The Gospel

debt? In fact, the Bible taught me that when I am angry because someone has wronged me, I need to forgive and not seek retaliation. Could I possibly be more charitable than God?

If it was God's justice that required a death, how could killing an innocent person—the only truly innocent person who ever lived—possibly be described as "justice"? And while we were careful to declare "salvation is by grace and not by human works," the fact is, believing in the right doctrines was the work we needed to do to be saved.

It finally came to the point I had to acknowledge, at least to myself and God, that I just did not believe the formula I had been taught as the gospel anymore. We often find ourselves wanting to believe something, but we know wanting to believe is not the same thing as actually believing it.

This doesn't mean I ever stopped believing in Jesus. I believe Jesus is the Son of God and Savior of the world. I have always known one of the most real and truthful moments of my life happened in that back pew. What I experienced there was real. Nor did I ever stop believing in the Troublemaker. It seems altogether possible that it was none other than the Troublemaker who was taking me through the hell of deconstruction. Isn't that what troublemakers do?

Make no mistake, deconstruction of our beliefs is hell. Or at least purgatory. But it is also the doorway to reconstructing our faith in a way that, being believable, works for us.

I read. I thought. I experienced deep depression. I prayed. I listened. Gradually a new understanding of what happened in the back pew of a little Methodist church began to grow and bloom.

The fluency I had developed in the language spoken by my elderly friend in the pew complicated the process of reshaping my belief in Jesus to something I could articulate as reasonable and true. The ways we speak about God are both powerful and confining. Spiritual phrases and words are filled with memory and implication beyond the meanings of the words themselves.

It was as if I had experienced God in a real way, but the words I was given to describe that encounter actually belonged to a different God. Yet, without such words I couldn't share my experience of God with anyone else. I needed words and concepts for faith to be communal, but those words and concepts came to define my faith rather than merely describing it. The ways we learn to talk about what we think and experience begin to become as real to us as the experience itself.

If this is true of sermons and books, it is even more true of songs. A particular understanding of Jesus and his death known as punitive substitutionary atonement is deeply embedded in evangelical language and culture. It is a painstaking and difficult task to deconstruct that language and replace it with a fuller understanding of the Passover mystery and why we need it.

My story of deconstruction and reconstruction is by no means unique. Over the past decade and a half, numerous evangelicals have similarly experienced deconstructing and reconstructing faith along these theological fault lines. As in the story of a tailor and his infamous emperor, once a few people start to question why the emperor is naked, it becomes obvious to more and more people that the emperor indeed has no clothes. This is how theological insight has always developed and evolved.

As I moved through my own deconstruction and reconstruction, as a pastor who had always valued sharing the gospel with other people, my biggest question became: What then is the gospel, the good news of Jesus? If a friend begins to wonder what it might mean to believe in the God of Jesus, or what it means to follow Jesus, what can I honestly tell them? What takes the place of the old gospel formula?

I am sorry to disappoint you, but I am not going to replace the old formula with a new and improved formula. A significant problem with the old formula is precisely that it is a formula. It reduces the depth of a relational and mystical experience with God to a logical set of ideas. A formulaic gospel reduces complex theological issues to a few simplified sound bites. Like the explanation I received from my lovely old friend in the back pew, such a formula may be easily relatable to those who already believe it but largely irrelevant and nonsensical to those who do not.

The Gospel

That said, the gospel, as I now understand it, has much in common with some of the ideas contained in the old formula. We do live in a broken, sinful world. We hurt each other, hurt the planet we share, and hurt the human community.

The reason we behave so hurtfully is simply that we have all been hurt and carry familiar wounds. This is how sin works. This is the principle behind original sin. It is not so much that I inherited a genetic tendency to sin that could be tracked back through the generations to Adam in the same way I inherited my blue eyes from my father and passed them on to my children.

My elders have all been wounded. Their wounds caused them to raise the next generation in ways that wounded us. We, in turn, have wounded the generations that come after us. Sin is passed from generation to generation. We wound because we are wounded.

While this is often a component of our primary relationships, it is far from personal or individual. Sin is systemic. It buries itself in our culture, politics, economies, and not least religion.

A theme that runs throughout our wounds is a belief in scarcity. In an unreflective way we are nurtured to believe that there is not enough for everyone. There is not enough food, not enough money, not enough safety. It is simply not possible for everyone to have all they need.

More importantly, there is not enough love, acceptance, or affection to fill our own needs, let alone to fill everyone's need to belong and be valued. Space is already crowded inside our walls. The mindset of scarcity allows us to think we have no affection or relational responsibility to share with those on the outside. There is not even enough of God's love for everyone. There is just adequate divine love to save people who believe in Jesus.

Given such scarcity, we can only succeed when others fail. We only win when someone else loses. This scarcity informs the old gospel formula: believe it now, because tomorrow may be too late! And for those who believe, if we don't go out and win souls, someone less benevolent will.

In a broader social context, even ideas of communalism quickly fall victim to selfishness and the exclusion of the other. We have a community that shares freely, but not with everyone. We love the whole world and want everyone to know about Jesus . . . so long as they stay where they are and don't crash our party or mess up our church.

Winners oppress losers. And the winners are always vastly outnumbered by the losers. This imbalance leaves the very few who make it to the winner's circle insecure and anxious. Winners know how easily they could be overcome by the vast expanse of losers. So we double down on oppression. We gather yet more wealth and power as a means of protecting ourselves from threat. The hurt and brokenness of the world increase exponentially.

I am convinced this worldview of scarcity and the pattern of consequent sin does not so much anger God as it grieves God. God loves us. As I would do for my own children, God would give anything to see us all well, happy, and fulfilled.

From the earliest pages of the Bible, God has been trying to show us an alternative way of being together. Despite the ways it destroys us, we keep resurrecting our human fear of scarcity and our strategies to offset the threat of someone taking what little we have.

Truthfully, it is not hard to make a very good argument for scarcity. Those who hold this worldview most strongly are convinced they are only being realistic. So many people in the world live in deep poverty. There is not enough of the world's resources to go around. Is the problem scarcity or inequity? Is there not enough to go around because relatively few have far, far more of the world's resources at their disposal than they could ever possibly use?

Those very few who inhabit the winner's circle are very adept at preserving civic, economic, religious, and cultural systems that deflect attention away from their own inequitable collection of resources by pointing the rest of us to some other enemy: someone easily identified as different from ourselves. God created this world with an amazing amount of beautiful diversity. Given such

The Gospel

diversity, it is not hard to categorize and define each other by our differences.

This drama is easily observed as it is played out on the global stage. But the competition for scarce acceptance and resources is played out just as fiercely in much smaller and more intimate ways. The first murder involved Cain and Abel, two brothers experiencing sibling rivalry. It should not escape our attention that their conflict was then played out through religious practices that differed only slightly.

One of the first pieces of God's creative design to be broken by the genesis of sin was the relationship between the genders. Despite equality in the image and likeness of God, God warned Eve that the outcome of the knowledge of good and evil would leave her in a precarious position. "Your desire shall be for your husband, and he shall rule over you" (Genesis 3:16 NRSV.) Patriarchy is not part of God's created order. Patriarchy is the direct result of sin and the product of sinfully broken relationships in the world.

In every way we were created for harmony: with God, with the earth, with each other, and within ourselves. Sin breaks every element of that harmony. The web woven by sin leaves us psychologically wounded, at war with each other, living on an exhausted and depleted planet, and either hiding from an angry God or discouraged into disbelieving there could even be such a thing as God.

The drama of Christ's life, death, resurrection, and ascension into heaven leaves us with the tools we need to rediscover and reassert the harmony of creation. Yes, we are wounded and we have inflicted wounds. Both experiences leave us with deep feelings of shame.

Guilt is an objective reality. Either we have done a particular wrong or we have not. Shame, on the other hand, is completely subjective. It is a feeling. It is what we feel when we ourselves don't seem to be enough. It is often, but not always, what we feel when we do wrong. Oddly enough, it is also often what we feel when someone wrongs us.

When a school child bullies a weaker classmate, the bully is guilty. But most of the time the bully does not feel shame. If they did, they would stop bullying people. It is the bullied child who feels shame: shame that they are powerless to protect themselves; shame that, somehow, they were worthy of being demeaned. Despite the best advice of adults, going to the authorities only adds to their feeling of not being enough and their sense of shame.

Almost universally, the one who is bullied seeks to resolve their shame by finding someone even weaker to bully. When we are collectively bullied as a tribe, nation, or people, if we can finally achieve our own place of power we invariably become oppressors. This is a way of resolving our anger and shame. It keeps turning sin's endless cycle of wounded people into people who wound others.

When bullies with wealth and power pay us too little for our labor, it is not very expensive for them to turn our anger toward people even more marginalized than we are, thereby providing us with someone we can bully too. It would make more sense for underpaid workers to become angry at the power structures that keep them poor and weak. But shame and pride make it easier to attack someone we can safely attack rather than risk trying to change what we may not be powerful enough to change.

The ways I wound others make psychological sense. My own wounds largely explain why I choose the particular wrongs and sins I choose. But my wounds don't provide an excuse, only an explanation. God's love, mercy, and forgiveness deal with the guilt. As God answers Jesus's plea for our forgiveness from the cross, our guilt is fully resolved. But that doesn't necessarily heal our shame.

There was no more humiliating way Jesus could die than to die on a cross in the Roman Empire. It is his humiliation that resolves our shame.

The gospel, the good news of Jesus, turns everything upside down. It is the great and strong who are able to suffer with courage and faith. It is no shame to suffer. It is no shame to be persecuted. It is, in fact, evidence of divine blessing.

The Gospel

> Blessed are you when people hate you, and when they exclude you, revile you, and defame you on account of the Son of Man. . . .
> But woe to you who are rich,
>   for you have received your consolation.
> Woe to you who are full now,
>   for you shall be hungry.
> Woe to you who are laughing now,
>   for you will mourn and weep. (Luke 6:22, 24–26 NRSV)

The cross unfolds for us how full, wide, and deep God's love for us is. It must be admitted, however, that for most of us who believe Christ is the means of our salvation, while this doctrine is fine in theory, we have little actual experience of such love. The messages we have been more likely to hear about God and why Jesus died on the cross leave us fearful and uncertain.

A thousand years ago a man named Anselm twisted the message of the cross to feature a God so angry he had to kill us if we sinned and so petty he didn't really care who he killed so long as his honor was reestablished by killing someone. Anselm believed we earn God's wrath through our sin. To save us from himself, God sent his son to punish in our place. Anselm left us with a God who acts like the bully of the universe. As with any bully, we find ourselves shamed by Anselm's God.

Unfortunately, Anselm's view of the cross was absorbed by both Western streams of Christianity: Roman Catholicism and Protestantism. This misunderstanding of the cross creates anxieties and attitudes that block the very harmonies Jesus died to renew.

A fuller understanding of the cross and the Passover mystery releases us from guilt and shame. We are able to know that God has loved and longed for us all along, without regard to what we believed or did. Like the father of the infamous prodigal son, God has always left the porch light on and kept the makings of a celebratory feast in the pantry in the event of our return home.

The cross, as Anselm explains it, does not so much provide forgiveness as it repays an obligation. It satisfies God's need to restore divine honor. Forgiveness would simply remove the obligation, as when a debt is forgiven. When we experience actual forgiveness, our own reactions to the people who sin against us are transformed. We come to realize that the most helpful thing we can do, even for ourselves, is to simply forgive without precondition.

Being forgiven by God, we are free to forgive. Rather than holding our anger until a future day of retribution, we can release our anger today through the gift of forgiveness. This implies a particular theology. Because of the Passover mystery, we can now believe in a God who, rather than holding his anger for a future day of retribution, simply forgives and welcomes us to his feast. We can, by believing in Christ, already sample the hors d'oeuvres God is serving now in the lobby before the doors open for the main meal.

But what of Jesus's woes to those who are rich and full now? Are they not going to suffer the pangs of hunger and poverty in a future day of retribution? There is an old joke about a wealthy man who asked to bring his riches to heaven. Converting everything he owned to gold, he filled a steamer trunk with gold bricks only to arrive in heaven to find he had spent his life accumulating paving stones.

God's feast is whatever God puts on the table. On that future day when Christ is fully revealed to the universe, those who believe they are rich and full now will realize the true poverty of their lives because they had been empty and dominated by scarcity all along. They will either gladly surrender their greed and pride of possession to join the feast or, clinging to what they thought they had, simply cease to be, for there is nothing at God's table they are willing to accept.

Let's add together all the elements of the Passover mystery: the Son of God being born a human body; the healing life and teaching of Jesus; his execution and burial, followed by his resurrection and ascension; and, finally, the coming of the Holy Spirit on Pentecost. These events become the actual tools we need to live as a newly created humanity in an old and broken world. As followers in the community of Jesus, we are taught and empowered to resist being pressed into the mold of the cultures around us.

The Gospel

We understand our inherited cultures have evolved in the broken world as we have seen it from what the apostle Paul called a human point of view.

We learn from Jesus how glory and greatness are found in serving one another for the common good and in emptying ourselves for the sake of the world. We know that a good and holy life consists of loving people the way God loves us all. Such love is not limited to our own people, family, or nation. Our neighborhood includes the stranger and even those we previously viewed as the enemy.

Such radical living is only possible when our human spirits are enlivened by the Spirit of God. This is not a new reality we are creating, by the way. It is the new creation God formed in the Passover mystery.

As a young man I briefly accepted and embraced the doctrine that speaking in tongues (the ability to speak and/or pray in a language we have not learned) is the true evidence of being filled with the Holy Spirit. That was only one of my many adventures in missing the point.

I now am inclined to say that the best display of the Holy Spirit is the genuine joy we find in being together with people of every nation, race, culture, gender, or economic status. The Spirit is found in celebrating with a fully diverse community the mighty things God has done for all of us. A church that is truly spiritual or Spirit-filled is a church that embraces diversity on collective and personal levels. This is the case not only in the pews on Sunday morning but equally in the boardroom and on the staff team.

It is only in the embrace of diversity that the healing of sin's disharmonies can begin. Churches might become large and prosperous through a strategy of focusing on a narrow demographic. But the cost of such strategy is true spirituality. Likewise, doctrines of separation, exclusion, and intolerance prevent us from living the good news of Jesus in the community that claims his name.

We could debate whether there is a true scarcity of the world's resources or whether the great poverty so many experience is attributable to the way we have allowed too few people to collect and hoard too much. But certainly we cannot argue that there is a true scarcity of God's love. To believe that God's grace is only given to those who believe what we believe about God and Jesus is to believe in a god who is far too small to be God.

The Passover mystery is our salvation. Jesus is "the way, the truth, and the life" (John 14:6 NRSV). With that proclaimed, there are more ways to Jesus than we can possibly imagine.

This, then, is the good news of Jesus: God is renewing the entire universe, having reconciled everything to himself in Christ. Within the Passover mystery that ties these events together, the cross shows us the danger and destruction of the violent and coercive paths we have been following and frees us from the wounds sin has inflicted on us, thereby freeing us from slavery to sin and death. The life and teaching of Jesus reveal what life in a new human community can and will be like. The Holy Spirit allows us to begin living that life with each other and God now.

Living in newness of life is not merely personal and individual. Life in the Spirit is collective and communal. It has deep social and political repercussions. These too are part of the good news of Jesus.

To believe and follow Jesus is to work against racism, economic inequity, military and economic imperialism, and environmental destruction. The good news of Jesus is not that we can go to heaven when we die. The good news of Jesus is that heaven has come to us, is coming to us even more fully, and we can begin living as an outpost of heaven right here, right now.

It would be wonderful to think that the church as a whole or the local organizations we call churches form this countercultural community that offers a taste of heaven. At her very best—which is exceedingly rare throughout history—the church does offer a glimpse of the relationships that make heaven what we hope.

But far too often culture has left more of an imprint on the church than the other way around. This is particularly true in places where long-standing Christendom has allowed the church to pursue and perpetuate theologies, philosophies, and

The Gospel

practices designed by the world's empires to protect themselves against scarcity.

If the church is to fully reflect the life of Christ in the world, she must be herself converted to a fuller understanding of the cross within the Passover mystery. We will abandon doctrines that divide one people from another, permit reckless plunder of the earth's resources, and constrict our ability to imagine the scope of God's love. A full understanding of the cross will call us to embrace God's mercy and provision for all God's creation.

My own beliefs are a mystery to me. I don't know why I believe all the things I believe. Some of my beliefs can surely be attributed to familial and social culture. But even my siblings, who sprouted from identical cultural soil, do not share all my beliefs. It would worry me if they did.

Sometimes I have tried to believe things I really did not believe because I thought I *should* believe those things, often because mentors and friends I trusted said they were true. Attempting to believe never has been healthy. It ends up merely pretending to believe.

My work as a pastor for more than forty years persuades me it is neither healthy nor helpful to try to talk people into believing something they do not. Pretending to believe is not the same thing as having faith.

That said, there is good news to be shared. Exposing people to possibilities, particularly when we express those possibilities by living in a manner consistent with what we believe, is always healthy and often helpful. Sharing the possibility of faith while actually living what we believe as fully as we can could well be the warm sunshine that allows a friend's own faith to grow within them.

So we expose the love of God to whomever we can, not in debate, but in living the command to love one another as Christ has loved us.

> From now on, therefore, we regard no one from a human point of view. . . . So if anyone is in Christ, there is a new creation: everything old has passed away, see, everything

has become new! All this is from God, who reconciled us to himself through Christ, and has given us the ministry of reconciliation; that is, in Christ God was reconciling the world to himself, not counting their trespasses against them, and entrusting the ministry of reconciliation to us.... Since God is making his appeal through us; we entreat you on behalf of Christ, be reconciled to God. (2 Corinthians 5:16–20 NRSV)

Bibliography

Bonhoeffer, Dietrich. *The Cost of Discipleship*. New York: Simon & Schuster, 1995.
Vermes, Geza. *The Authentic Gospel of Jesus*. Westminster: Allen Lane, 2003.

www.ingramcontent.com/pod-product-compliance
Lightning Source LLC
Chambersburg PA
CBHW070248100426
42743CB00011B/2178